# VEGAN
# BBQ

# ·VEGAN·
# ·BBQ·

## KATY BESKOW

70 delicious plant-based
recipes to cook outdoors

Photography by
Luke Albert

*Hardie Grant*

QUADRILLE

**Publishing Director**
Sarah Lavelle

**Commissioning Editor**
Harriet Webster

**Copy Editor**
Clare Sayer

**Art Direction & Design**
Emily Lapworth

**Photographer**
Luke Albert

**Food Stylist**
Tamara Vos

**Prop Stylist**
Louie Waller

**Make-up Artist**
Dani Hooker

**Head of Production**
Stephen Lang

**Production Controller**
Nikolaus Ginelli

First published in 2022 by Quadrille,
an imprint of Hardie Grant Publishing

Quadrille
52–54 Southwark Street
London SE1 1UN
quadrille.com

Text © Katy Beskow 2022
Photography © Luke Albert 2022
Design and layout © Quadrille 2022

ISBN: 978 1 78713 860 5

Printed in China

# ON THE GRILL 28

# SIZZLING SIDES 68

# SALADS & EXTRAS 104

# SWEET TREATS 130

# INTRODUCTION

'What do vegans eat at a barbecue?' is a question that I've been asked, and overheard (as a vegan of 15 years), more times than I can count. Barbecuing and grilling are traditionally associated with cooking meats, and aside from a simple skewer of vegetables or a corn-on-the-cob, the options have previously been limited. But the truth is that barbecuing combines a range of techniques to bring out the best in so many vegetables and plant-based foods – making them the stars of the show!

When you move away from the idea that the barbecue is just there to cook meat (or processed meat alternatives) a world of possibilities opens up to you. Ingredients are transformed when cooked on the barbecue, with charred, smoky flavours and crisp yet tender textures to awaken your senses. I believe that everything tastes better when it's cooked on the barbecue so you can really push the boundaries and be creative! Using fresh, sustainably grown, seasonal ingredients that are readily available in supermarkets, it's easy to create outstanding food, whether that's standalone suppers or feasts for gatherings of friends and family.

Hosting a barbecue for loved ones is one of life's little pleasures. Unlike cooking in a cramped kitchen, cooking outdoors feels particularly sociable as you can enjoy the company of others, a cool drink, and making memories while you cook full-of-flavour food, hopefully in the sunshine. It's also a great way to showcase vegan food in a casual and relaxed way. But don't just limit your barbecue to a once-a-year piece of equipment that grills vegan burgers and plant-based sausages; use it more often to cook your supper, without any special occasion needed.

Cooking can feel like a chore. Weekly meals on repeat (even for me, as a food writer) can leave us uninspired by yet another supper to prepare. This is when it's time to dust off the barbecue, add some fire (literally), cook outside, and infuse your food with flavours that can't be created in any other way. I'm a big believer that barbecuing isn't just for those glorious summer get-togethers, but something that can be enjoyed all year round, as long as you avoid those rainy days. On a chilly autumn or winter day (or evening), simply grab your hat and a warm coat, fire up the barbecue and be inspired by seasonal produce to invigorate your meals.

Whether you're a vegan, vegetarian, or are simply craving fresh new dishes, there are so many delicious possibilities when barbecuing plant-based foods. Not only are you choosing more sustainable, cruelty-free and seasonal ingredients, but you're opening up a world of new flavours. There are also far fewer food safety concerns when cooking vegan food on the barbecue compared to cooking animal products, so you won't have to worry about the serious risks of feeding your friends and family undercooked meat – a real plus if you are new to this type of cooking.

If you're not confident with preparing or cooking on the barbecue, I've included tips and advice on the types of barbecue and charcoal to use, how to light it effectively, any extra equipment you need, and practical ways to know if your barbecue is hot enough (or too hot) to cook with. I promise that it's much simpler than you think. I've included a shopping guide of my favourite ingredients, and every recipe has a 'Hot Tip' to help you get the most out of the ingredients. Most of the recipes are cooked on the barbecue itself, but I've included some additional recipes that are cooked or prepared in the kitchen; these are dishes that perfectly complement barbecued food, so you can create something memorable every time. I've kept the recipes as simple as possible, while packing in masses of flavour, so you can spend more time eating and less time preparing.

Have fun as you cook in the great outdoors – whether it's on your bijou balcony, garden patio, or even on the beach – while you enrich your food with depth of flavour and perfect, crisp textures. There's something exciting about cooking outside on the barbecue, with that rich smoke, the sizzling sounds from the grill and a varied way of cooking that will inspire you to create some of your best vegan food that everyone will love.

# HOW TO USE THIS BOOK

Refresh or learn how to get the best from your barbecue in these initial introductory pages, which include information on:

- Choosing a barbecue to suit your needs
- Which charcoal to use
- How to successfully light the barbecue
- How to determine the varying temperatures of your barbecue
- Useful outdoor cooking equipment
- Ingredients for the best ever vegan barbecue

I've also put together 10 menus of dishes that work well together, for every occasion and season. Feel free to choose and combine your favourite recipes, or use these time-saving menu plans.

There are four chapters of recipes in this book:

## ON THE GRILL

Use this chapter to choose your main dishes, all cooked on the barbecue. The dishes require some kitchen preparation time before they hit the grill, most of which can be done in advance. Follow the temperature guides for fail-safe dishes. From mushroom masala sausages (page 64) to smoky paella with butter beans and olives (page 36), there's something for everyone!

## SIZZLING SIDES

Find your favourite side dishes to accompany the main event, or prepare one or two of these recipes if you require something lighter. From tasty dishes you can serve as a starter to classic barbecue sides, bring some variety to your plate with these recipes. Most of these are cooked on the grill, but some are cooked in the kitchen and are labelled with 'From the kitchen'.

## SALADS & EXTRAS

What's a barbecue without a fresh salad, dips and sauces? These recipes have been created to sit alongside main and side dishes, and deliver on freshness and texture. Some are cooked on the barbecue, the rest are whipped up in the kitchen and have been labelled 'From the kitchen' for your convenience.

## SWEET TREATS

Indulge in a sweet treat (or two) from this chapter. From barbecue banoffee pie (page 132) to sangria (page 148), choose recipes to cook on the grill, or pick treats prepared in the kitchen that will save you time and finish your barbecue in the sweetest way.

# THE BARBECUE

## CHARCOAL BARBECUES

My choice of barbecue is always charcoal, for the following reasons:

- Exceptional and unique flavour that is 'cooked' into the food
- Versatility of the cooking methods you can use
- Lower purchase cost
- The way it connects you with your food, building confidence and skill every time you barbecue.

Cooking on a charcoal barbecue can take a little practice and some patience to maintain the perfect cooking temperature, but the unique results are worth the wait. Charcoal barbecues come in a range of sizes, making them suitable for smaller spaces and for easier storage. If you're keen to get the most out of a charcoal barbecue, it's worth choosing a model that has a lid as this controls the temperature and creates an 'outdoor oven' as the heat circulates to cook the food, which is particularly useful when you need low temperatures to cook produce like root vegetables. Some charcoal barbecues have vents, which help to control the intensity of the temperature; the more the vents are open, the hotter the barbecue will become; when they are closed, less oxygen can access the charcoal, meaning it will burn slower and for longer at a lower temperature. Simple charcoal barbecue grills are effective and versatile for simple recipes, proving that there's no need to go to lots of expense as a beginner or less frequent barbecue user.

Avoid disposable charcoal barbecues, if possible; they produce large quantities of non-recyclable materials that end up in landfill, as well as generally using poor charcoal and lighter fuels that can taint the flavour of your food. Instead, I'd recommend a small, portable charcoal barbecue that can be cleaned and reused, and you can then choose the quality and sustainability of the charcoal used. More often than not, I use my smaller portable charcoal barbecue grill as it's quick and easy to set up, and is large enough to cook exactly the quantities I need for a meal without needing to replenish the charcoal.

## GAS GRILLS

Gas grills are often larger in size, more expensive to purchase and have limited cooking methods, compared with charcoal barbecues. Although it's tempting to splurge on a bells-and-whistles gas grill to stand proudly on a patio, it's worth noting that gas burns at a lower temperature than charcoal, so it's more difficult to create that smoky flavour and those tender textures. However, you can be ready to cook in less time and be more precise with temperature variations, and are often able to cook larger quantities of food at the same time. The clean-up is often easier too.

# THE FUEL

The type of charcoal you choose has an effect on the intensity of the heat, the length of the burn and the flavour that is transmitted, but aside from trying them all, it often comes down to personal preference and availability. Avoid 'instant light' charcoal or briquettes where possible, as they contain unnecessary chemicals that can tarnish the taste of your food.

## LUMPWOOD CHARCOAL

Good-quality lumpwood charcoal is natural and sustainable, and is my charcoal of choice as it delivers an exceptional smoky flavour every time. It also gives off that nostalgic and recognizable 'wood smoke' aroma! Lumpwood charcoal reaches a high temperature quickly and easily, and burns through descending temperatures in total for around an hour, giving you plenty of time to cook a variety of dishes that require different temperatures. You'll need to top up the charcoal and allow it to heat through if you require higher temperatures for a longer time, so a little patience is required.

## BRIQUETTES

Charcoal briquettes are a popular choice as they are readily available to purchase. They are great for barbecue beginners as they burn at a more consistent temperatures and for longer than lumpwood charcoal, without cooling too quickly. They are made from compressed wood, often processed with some additives that aid in the longer and consistent heat time. They are a great choice when you require a consistent and longer cooking temperature and time, especially if you're cooking for lots of people and you don't want to top up the fuel.

## NATURAL FIRELIGHTERS

Everyone has their preferred method of lighting a barbecue. For me, it's using natural firelighter cubes. These cubes are made of compressed wood and create the flames needed to heat the charcoal. There are many brands and types of firelighters available, so opt for ones that are free from additives and lighter fuel to avoid any flavour tainting or unnecessary chemicals.

**HOT TIP**

For extra flavour, soak a bunch of fresh, woody herbs (such as thyme, rosemary and sage) in water for 15 minutes, then add to the hot embers before grilling. You can also burn additional wood with the embers including hickory and oak (for flavours that pack a punch!) or milder applewood or beech.

# HOW TO LIGHT AND COOK ON YOUR BARBECUE

Follow these steps to make lighting your barbecue successful every time.

## 1. GET AHEAD

On average, it takes between 20–35 minutes for charcoal to reach the perfect temperature for hot, direct grilling, so fire up the barbecue in good time so it is at the optimum temperature range for your recipes. Read through the recipes first to plan how long you'll need to spend preparing in the kitchen and make a plan of the cooking order, including the temperature ranges required.

## 2. SAFETY

Set up your barbecue in an open space, away from any hanging branches and a distance from wooden fences. Ensure the barbecue is positioned on a solid surface and is not wobbling. Keep children and animal companions at a safe distance from the barbecue as you start the set-up to avoid accidents or injuries. Have some heatproof gloves nearby, and a domestic fire blanket large enough to cover the barbecue is recommended in the event of an emergency.

## 3. CHARCOAL CHOICES

Choose your preferred charcoal (lumpwood or briquettes) and consider how much you will need for the size and shape of barbecue you are using (individual guides are available in the manufacturer's instructions). Remember that larger amounts of charcoal will create hotter temperatures as it sits closer to the grill.

## 4. LIGHT

A lighter chimney is an easy-to-use and cost-effective piece of equipment that makes lighting a barbecue so much easier (and quicker) than the standard method. Scoop the charcoal into the lighter chimney, which is like a tall metal cylinder, then light 2–4 natural firelighters on the base grate of your barbecue. Place the device upright over the lit firelighters and allow the charcoal to ignite (the chimney will draw in oxygen from the base of the cylinder. When the top embers are grey with ash (in around 10–15 minutes), carefully pour all of them into the barbecue, and arrange as required for the recipe. If you don't have a lighter chimney, arrange the charcoal in a stack over the base grate, arrange and light 4–5 natural firelighters within the charcoal. Allow the flames to settle and let the embers become grey with ash in around 20–30 minutes, then arrange as required by the recipe.

## 5. PLACE THE GRILL

Carefully secure the grill in place over the hot embers and heat for 10–15 minutes more. When food touches the hot grill, it should sizzle.

# TEMPERATURES

Get more from your grill by using these methods to control the temperature. It's good to use your senses and instincts to know when the embers are suitable for cooking, when they are too hot, and how and when to cook with cooler temperatures.

## HOW DO I KNOW HOW HOT MY BARBECUE IS?

Notice the colour changes on the embers, with glowing white ash and bright red middles indicating a high heat. Each stage lasts about 10–12 minutes (if you don't add extra charcoal), but factors such as opening vents on the barbecue, and the weather and temperature of the environment can affect this. You can also estimate the temperature by carefully holding the palm of your hand 5cm (2in) above the middle of the grill.

**Flames are visible and most of the coals are black or grey**

Wait until the flames die down. Be patient at this stage – it's worth the wait.

**Embers are glowing white and have bright red middles**

This is a high heat. You can hold your palm comfortably 5cm (2in) above grill for 1–2 seconds.

**Embers are ashy white with some red glow**

This is a medium heat. You can hold your palm comfortably 5cm (2in) above grill for 3–4 seconds.

**Embers are yellow-brown with no red glow**

This is a low heat. You can hold your palm comfortably 5cm (2in) above grill for 5–6 seconds.

## DIRECT HEAT

This is traditional barbecue grilling with an even layer of embers arranged under the grill. Direct heat is very hot initially and will cool evenly over time. Direct heat is perfect for searing food quickly, while keeping moisture through the middle, which is perfect for foods that taste great with a little charring, including teriyaki tofu with charred greens (page 33) and heritage tomato bruschetta (page 74).

## INDIRECT HEAT

Push the embers to one side of the barbecue to create an area of the barbecue suitable for indirect heat. The area will remain warm, but without the direct heat of the embers beneath. This is useful to keep cooked foods warm until you are ready to enjoy them, but also to cook foods at a lower temperature for longer including buttered hasselback squash with chimichurri (page 47) and brown sugar beans (page 78).

# COOKING EQUIPMENT

Alongside your barbecue, domestic fire safety equipment and charcoal, it's useful to have a few utensils to hand to make the process easier and so you can cook a variety of barbecue dishes.

## Tongs

Long-handled tongs are essential for turning food on the hot grill, as well as placing and removing cooked foods from the grill, and rearranging embers. I'd recommend tongs of at least 35cm (14in) in length to avoid burning your hand; also consider the materials used for durability and heatproofing on the handles.

## Kitchen foil

Use kitchen foil to envelop ingredients that you wish to steam on the barbecue. I usually double-wrap to avoid any leakage and ensure even cooking.

## Skewers

Skewers are an essential piece of barbecue equipment, as they make turning small chunks and multiple ingredients easy with less risk of them falling through the grill. The cooking is often more even, and food served this way looks great too! Reusable metal skewers are my choice, as they often have a sharper point that makes threading firmer vegetables like onion and potato easier. Wooden bamboo skewers work well too, but do remember to soak them in water for 30 minutes before using.

## Barbecue-safe pan

Cooking one-pot dishes such as paella on the barbecue is easy with a barbecue-safe carbon steel pan that is versatile enough to use in the kitchen too. Use the pan for dishes that require sauces or added liquid, and simply place directly onto the hot grill. In this book, the recipes that require a barbecue-safe pan are all made in a 30cm (12in) carbon steel paella pan.

## Pizza stone

The barbecue can be used to make a great quality pizza, with a crispy base and a smoky flavour. Pizza stones are a relatively inexpensive piece of equipment that can be used for many years – they make the pizza base extra crisp and bubbly by drawing out excess moisture from the dough as it cooks.

## Basting brush

Choose a long-handled basting brush for oiling or coating with extra marinade during cooking. This stops the ingredients from sticking to the grill, or drying out during longer cooking times.

# YOUR BARBECUE
# SHOPPING TROLLEY

## FRESH PRODUCE

### Fruit, vegetables and herbs

Let vegetables be the stars of the show, bringing colour, texture, crunch, variety, seasonality and excitement to any barbecue feast. Root vegetables, such as onions, carrots, potatoes and butternut squash, become tender and sweet when barbecued, with caramelized flavours. Lighter vegetables, such as sugarsnap peas, broccoli, courgette (zucchini), fennel and tomatoes, become charred and absorb the smokiness of the charcoal and take less time to cook than root vegetables. Shop seasonally to find the best-quality produce, as well as keeping your choices varied throughout the year with different vegetables.

Seasonal fruits are versatile enough to use for barbecued desserts, such as hot balsamic strawberries (page 145) but also make contrasting, juicy additions to many savoury dishes like pulled mango tacos with beans, radishes and coriander (page 43). Grilling fruits intensifies their flavour and locks in mouth-watering juices, so don't be afraid to cook up your favourite fruits for unexpected (and delicious) results. I particularly love the transformation after barbecuing wedges of watermelon – it develops a meaty, succulent texture that works wonderfully in grilled watermelon with Thai green curry (page 67). Citrus fruits are a quick and easy way to add a burst of freshness to grilled foods but make sure you choose unwaxed lemons, limes and oranges as waxed varieties may be glazed with a product from an animal source.

Use fresh leafy herbs including basil, flat-leaf parsley and coriander (cilantro) to instantly lift the flavours of a dish. Store them stem down in a glass of water for longevity.

### Tofu

Extra-firm tofu is wonderful when grilled on the barbecue, creating a crisp outer and tender middle, while naturally absorbing a smoked flavour. Pre-pressed extra-firm tofu is available in supermarkets and saves extra preparation, but if this is unavailable, simply wrap the tofu in kitchen paper or a clean, dry tea towel and place on a large plate. Place another plate on top of the block and add a couple of cookbooks or a heavy pan on top to weigh it down. Allow to stand for 1 hour before slicing the tofu into the desired pieces. Silken tofu is silky and creamy, making it perfect to use in desserts such as chocolate mousse with smoked salt (page 139). Silken tofu does not require pressing.

# NON-DAIRY

## Milks

There's a wide range of plant-based milks in supermarkets, including oat, almond and rice. I find the most versatile plant-based milk is unsweetened soya, which can be used in savoury and sweet dishes. In this book, coconut milk refers to the thick, canned variety found in the ambient aisles of supermarkets.

## Cheeses

No barbecue is complete without some cheese to melt over your grilled foods! Vegan cheeses have improved vastly over the years, so choose a variety that suits the recipe and your tastes. I prefer hard vegan cheese with a coconut base, and soft vegan cream cheeses with an almond base – both available in supermarkets. Try it in grilled cheese and pico de gallo quesadillas (page 38).

## Vegan butter

I used salted vegan butter, sold in blocks, when creating these recipes. Remember that vegan butter and dairy-free margarines can vary in oil content, so you may need to adjust the quantities used. An essential for buttered hasselback squash with chimichurri (page 47).

## Yogurt

Vegan yogurt is versatile for both sweet and savoury barbecued dishes and is perfect for marinades and cooling dips. Thick coconut varieties and plain unsweetened soya yogurt offer the most versatility.

## Cream

Soya or oat-based single (light) and double (heavy) creams are widely available in supermarkets and can be used in the same way as their dairy counterparts.

## Mayonnaise

Vegan mayonnaise is a great addition to your store cupboard for dipping, spreading and dressing. Choose from a variety of brands, with added flavours, if you like.

# AMBIENT

## Spices and blends

Keep a good supply of ground spices and dried herbs available to pack in flavour. Pre-blended spice mixes and pastes, including curry paste, Chinese five-spice and jerk seasoning, offer speedy and simple additions without having to blend the spices yourself. Make sure that any curry pastes are vegan by checking the label before you buy.

## Oil

Oil prevents ingredients sticking to the hot grill bars, so it's important that it's brushed over food before you place it on the grill. I use either sunflower oil or a light olive oil for brushing and cooking as their mild flavours won't affect the taste of the food. Extra virgin olive oil is ideal for dressing salads when a richer flavour is required.

## Canned beans

Canned beans are easy to store, quick to cook with, and versatile enough to use for many dishes on and off the barbecue. Canned butter (lima) beans, black beans, red kidney beans and cannellini beans add protein and extra substance to smoky paella with butter beans and olives (page 36) and in peanut butter and chilli jam bean burgers with pretzels (page 55). Give the beans a thorough rinse before use to remove any 'canned' taste, and pat dry to remove moisture when adding to burgers so they hold and bind.

## Plant-based meat alternatives

There are many excellent plant-based meat alternatives to beef burgers, pork sausages, chicken breasts and steak now readily available from supermarkets. Although none of the recipes in this book uses meat alternatives as ingredients, feel free to add your favourite plant-based meat alternative to the grill to enjoy alongside these dishes.

# VEGAN BARBECUE MENUS

The joy of a barbecue feast is throwing together a range of mix and match dishes for everyone to enjoy, or use one of these menus for simple theming and fuss-free planning.

## MENU 1

Tamarind aubergines (page 30)

Olive flatbreads (page 75)

Pistachio, pomegranate and mint salad with bulgar and orange (page 119)

Dukkah (page 124)

Sticky figs with maple-candied walnuts and pomegranate (page 140)

## MENU 2

Peanut butter and chilli jam bean burgers with pretzels (page 55)

Candy-stripe onions (page 98)

Brown sugar beans (page 78)

Deli pickle mayo (page 128)

Barbecue banoffee pie (page 132)

## MENU 3

Sweet and sour tofu and pineapple (page 34)

Satay Tenderstem, courgette, baby corns and sugarsnaps (page 35)

Nutty rice salad (page 117)

Crunchy sesame and lime salad with soy and edamame (page 116)

Grilled asparagus with orange and black pepper (page 80)

## MENU 4

Sizzling fajitas with charred lime (page 54)

Grilled cheese and pico de gallo quesadillas (page 38)

Grilled guacamole (page 129)

Coriander butter corn on the cob with lime (page 83)

Tortilla turnovers with hot cinnamon apples (page 144)

## MENU 5

Stone-baked pizzas (page 49)

Mediterranean sausages (page 48)

Heritage tomato bruschetta (page 74)

Italian baked beans (page 90)

Grilled lemon cake with limoncello cream and pistachios (page 135)

## MENU 6

Smoky paella with butter beans and olives (page 36)

Fire-roasted tomato gazpacho (page 70)

Salt and vinegar Padron peppers (page 87)

Barbecue patatas bravas (page 86)

Sangria (page 148)

## MENU 7

Grill-side katsu burger with wasabi mayo (page 62)

Quick pink pickles (page 125)

Teriyaki tofu with charred greens (page 33)

Sticky broccoli with soy, chilli and sesame (page 79)

Grilled and pickled baby cucumbers (page 121)

## MENU 8

Buttered hasselback squash with chimichurri (page 47)

Ratatouille foil parcels (page 91)

Sage and onion sausage rolls with ketchup (page 102)

Warm grapes with whipped cream cheese and chives (page 112)

Chocolate mousse with smoked salt (page 139)

## MENU 9

Mushroom masala sausages (page 64)

Spiced yogurt cauliflower and mango (page 44)

Garlic naan breads (page 94)

Carrot, coriander and toasted cashew salad (page 114)

Chocolate fondue (page 134)

## MENU 10

Smoked sweet potato chilli with chocolate and cinnamon (page 39)

Squash, apple and chestnut mushroom skewers with thyme oil (page 59)

Salt-baked potatoes (page 82)

Pecan and apple salad with charred carrots (page 95)

Cinder toffee (page 143)

# ·ON THE· ·GRILL·

# TAMARIND AUBERGINES

**BARBECUE COOKING
TEMPERATURE:** high heat

**SERVES** 2

My favourite way to cook aubergines is on the barbecue, as the skin absorbs all the smoky flavours and the flesh becomes ultra-tender. This recipe is simple and quick, but looks impressive served to your guests (or for your supper). Tamarind has a sour flavour that balances the sweet, smoked aubergines with hints of maple, cinnamon and chilli in the marinade. Serve with olive flatbreads (page 75) and pistachio, pomegranate and mint salad with bulgar and orange (page 119).

4 tbsp olive oil, plus extra
    for drizzling
3 tbsp maple syrup
2 tsp tamarind paste
½ tsp ground cinnamon
pinch of dried chilli flakes
2 aubergines (eggplants),
    halved lengthways with
    green top left intact
seeds of ½ pomegranate
handful of fresh flat-leaf
    parsley, chopped

Also pictured on pages 76–77

**1** In a bowl, whisk together the olive oil, maple syrup, tamarind paste, cinnamon and chilli flakes.

**2** Lay the aubergine halves on a flat surface and score the flesh in diagonal lines to make a criss-cross pattern. Dip the cut sides into the marinade, using a pastry brush to push the marinade into the scored lines, then coat the skin in the marinade. Stand the aubergines on a plate for 10–15 minutes, keeping the extra marinade in the bowl.

**3** Use tongs to place the aubergines onto the grill, skin-side down, for 15 minutes. Baste the flesh with extra marinade, then turn cut-side down onto the grill and cook for 10 minutes until browned and tender.

**4** Remove from the grill and arrange on a serving plate. Drizzle with a little extra olive oil, then scatter with pomegranate seeds and chopped parsley.

### HOT TIP

Aubergines absorb lots of flavour and moisture in a short space of time so there's no need to marinate longer than 15 minutes.

# TERIYAKI TOFU
## WITH CHARRED GREENS

**BARBECUE COOKING TEMPERATURE:**
medium heat

**SERVES** 4

Tofu is marinated in a sweet, salty and sticky sauce in this succulent dish, then served with charred greens. Teriyaki sauce is made for grilling, as it adds moisture as well as the perfect balance of sweet and very savoury. Prepare the sauce in advance as it will thicken slightly as it cools, creating the perfect glaze for tender tofu.

100ml (scant ½ cup) soy sauce

2 tbsp brown sugar

1 tbsp maple syrup

1 tbsp mirin

2 garlic cloves, crushed

1cm (½in) piece of ginger, peeled and grated

pinch of dried chilli flakes

280g (9oz) block of pre-pressed extra-firm tofu (see page 20), sliced horizontally into 4

12 florets of Tenderstem broccoli

16 sugarsnap peas

¼ savoy cabbage, cut into 4 wedges

½ tbsp sunflower oil, for brushing

1 tsp sesame seeds

Also pictured on pages 122–123

**1** Put the soy sauce, brown sugar, maple syrup, mirin, garlic, ginger and chilli flakes into a pan. Heat over a medium heat on the hob for 5–6 minutes until the mixture is bubbling, then remove from the heat and allow to cool and thicken for a few minutes.

**2** Blot the slices of tofu with kitchen paper or a clean cloth to remove any excess moisture. Score the tofu lightly in criss-cross pattern on one side (this will help the tofu to absorb the marinade). Place the tofu slices into a deep dish, then pour over the teriyaki marinade. Allow to stand for 1 hour, turning the tofu a couple of times.

**3** Skewer the broccoli florets, sugarsnap peas and cabbage wedges onto 4 metal skewers, with 3 pieces of broccoli, 4 sugarsnap peas and a wedge of cabbage on each. Brush with a little sunflower oil.

**4** Shake excess marinade off the tofu, then carefully place on the hot grill. Cook for 4–5 minutes on each side, turning when the cooked side appears firm.

**5** Add the loaded skewers to the hot grill and cook for 4–5 minutes, turning frequently until tender and charred.

**6** Remove the tofu slices from the grill and place on serving plates. Scatter each one with a few sesame seeds. Remove the skewers from the grill and carefully slide the vegetables onto the plates, placing the broccoli florets on top of the teriyaki tofu.

**HOT TIP**

Mirin is a sweet Japanese rice wine, which adds a little acidity to a dish, but less than vinegar. It's a great ingredient to keep in the cupboard for the perfect teriyaki sauce, noodle soups and fresh salad dressings. You'll find it in small bottles in most supermarkets.

# SWEET AND SOUR TOFU AND PINEAPPLE

**BARBECUE COOKING TEMPERATURE:**
medium heat

**SERVES** 4

Sticky, sweet and sour sauce, charred tofu and chunky pineapple – it's a match made in heaven, and even better when grilled over charcoal to enhance that smoky, deep flavour. Serve with satay Tenderstem, courgette, baby corns and sugarsnaps (page 35) and crunchy sesame and lime salad with soy and edamame (page 116).

6 tbsp tomato ketchup

3 tbsp soft brown sugar

1 tbsp soy sauce

1 tbsp sunflower oil

2 tsp malt vinegar

2 x 280g (9oz) blocks of pre-pressed extra-firm tofu (see page 20), chopped into chunky bite-sized pieces

1 pineapple, peeled, cored and chopped into chunky bite-sized pieces

**1** In a pan on the hob, stir together the ketchup, sugar, soy sauce, sunflower oil and malt vinegar. Pour in 50ml (scant ¼ cup) cold water, then cook over a low-medium heat for 10 minutes, stirring frequently to avoid sticking.

**2** Place the chunks of tofu and pineapple into a large bowl, then stir in the sweet and sour marinade. Coat the chunks in the marinade and allow to stand at room temperature for 1 hour.

**3** Slide the chunks of tofu and pineapple onto metal skewers, shaking off any excess marinade. Don't discard the bowl of marinade, as this will be used to baste the skewers when they are on the barbecue.

**4** Carefully place the skewers onto the barbecue and cook for 10–12 minutes, turning four times, to cook each surface until browned. Brush over a little extra sweet and sour marinade with each turn to pack the kebabs with flavour and avoid sticking.

**5** Remove from the heat and carefully slide the cooked tofu and pineapple off the metal skewers onto serving plates.

**HOT TIP**

Buy extra-firm tofu that has been pre-pressed, then simply blot away any additional moisture with kitchen paper or a clean cloth. If you have extra-firm tofu that is not pre-pressed, read my short guide on how to press tofu on page 20.

# SATAY TENDERSTEM, COURGETTE, BABY CORNS AND SUGARSNAPS

**BARBECUE COOKING TEMPERATURE:**
medium

**SERVES** 4

Barbecued vegetables develop layers of smoky and charred flavours, becoming crisp in some places. Smooth and gently spiced satay sauce works perfectly to balance this, adding richness and a silky texture. This dish has been the star of my barbecue on many occasions!

1 courgette (zucchini), sliced thickly into 12 half-rounds
12 stems of Tenderstem broccoli
12 sugarsnap peas
4 baby corns, each cut into 3 even pieces
1 tbsp sunflower oil

For the satay sauce
2 tbsp smooth peanut butter
1 tbsp sunflower oil
1 tbsp soy sauce
½ tsp Chinese five-spice
pinch of dried chilli flakes

**1** Thread the courgette, broccoli, sugarsnap peas and baby corns onto 4 skewers, aiming for 3 pieces of each vegetable on each. Brush generously with sunflower oil and set aside for a few moments.

**2** In a bowl, whisk together the peanut butter, sunflower oil, soy sauce, Chinese five-spice and chilli flakes with 50ml (scant ¼ cup) cold water until a smooth sauce is created.

**3** Carefully place the skewers onto the hot grill and cook for 5 minutes, turning a couple of times.

**4** Use a basting brush to generously smooth over the satay sauce (you may need to whisk in a tablespoon or two of extra cold water if the satay sauce has thickened while it was standing), covering all surfaces of the vegetables, then cook for a further 8–10 minutes until golden and tender.

**5** Carefully remove the vegetables from the skewers and serve.

**HOT TIP**

Skewer the chopped baby corns widthways through the tender core, as the vegetable can be too tender and fragile when threaded vertically.

# SMOKY PAELLA
## WITH BUTTER BEANS AND OLIVES

**BARBECUE COOKING TEMPERATURE:**
high heat

**SERVES** 4

The barbecue is the perfect place to cook paella as the heat starts high – perfect for chargrilling the vegetables – before naturally reducing in temperature while the rice is absorbing the saffron stock. It is also a wonderful, sociable way to cook this summery dish, which is just made for sharing. Use a deep, stainless steel paella dish and the freshest ingredients you can find. I love tender Spanish butter beans (from a jar rather than a can) for this recipe, and a pinch of good-quality saffron for a honeyed taste. Serve with a cool glass of sangria (page 148), and dream of a balmy, Spanish dusk.

pinch of saffron strands

800ml (3⅓ cups) hot vegetable stock

6 mixed mini sweet (bell) peppers, halved and deseeded

1 courgette (zucchini), sliced into rounds

2 tbsp olive oil

1 unwaxed lemon, halved

1 onion, finely diced

3 garlic cloves, crushed

1 tsp smoked paprika

1 tsp dried oregano

300g (10oz) bomba paella rice

400g (14oz) canned or jarred butter (lima) beans, drained and rinsed

8 pitted green olives, sliced into rounds

handful of fresh flat-leaf parsley, chopped

small handful of fresh dill, roughly torn, stems discarded

pinch of sea salt

Also pictured on pages 28 and 88–89

**1** Stir the saffron into the hot vegetable stock in a jug or pan and allow to infuse.

**2** In a bowl, toss together the peppers and courgettes with 1 tablespoon of the olive oil. Lay the vegetables onto the hot grill along with the lemon halves and cook for 2–3 minutes on each side, or until char lines appear and the vegetables soften. Set aside in a bowl.

**3** Drizzle the remaining tablespoon of olive oil into a 30cm (12in) carbon steel (barbecue-safe) paella pan (page 19) and place the pan onto the grill. When the oil is hot, add the diced onion and soften for 5–7 minutes.

**4** Add the garlic, smoked paprika and oregano and cook for a further 3–5 minutes, stirring frequently, until fragrant.

**5** Stir in the rice and coat in the mixture for a couple of minutes, then add in half the stock. Cover the pan with kitchen foil or close the barbecue lid and cook for 15–20 minutes, or until most of the stock has absorbed. Stir in the remaining stock along with the butter beans and cook for a further 10 minutes until the stock is absorbed and the dish is starchy and thickened.

**6** Scatter the cooked vegetables over the top and squeeze over the charred lemons. Scatter on the olives, flat-leaf parsley and dill. Season with salt to taste, then allow to stand off the heat for 5–10 minutes before eating.

### HOT TIP

Prepare all the ingredients before you start cooking so you can easily throw together the paella outside on the barbecue, with everything you need to hand.

# GRILLED CHEESE
## AND PICO DE GALLO QUESADILLAS

**BARBECUE COOKING TEMPERATURE:**
medium-high heat

**SERVES** 2

Fire up the barbecue and grill these moreish quesadillas, loaded with melted vegan cheese and fresh, tangy pico de gallo. The recipe is easy to double (or more), and feel free to add in some rinsed, canned red kidney beans for extra bite. Delicious when served with cooling slices of avocado, or a dip of deli pickle mayo (page 128).

4 large, firm tomatoes, diced
1 small red onion, finely diced
handful of fresh coriander (cilantro), finely chopped
juice of ½ unwaxed lime
pinch of smoked sea salt
4 large soft tortilla wraps
150g (5oz) hard vegan cheese, grated
1 tbsp olive oil

**1** Make the pico de gallo by combining the tomatoes, red onion, coriander, lime juice and smoked sea salt in a bowl. Allow to infuse for 1 hour.

**2** Lay out the tortilla wraps on a flat surface. Sprinkle one half of each tortilla with grated cheese, then spoon over the pico de gallo. Fold the tortillas in half (into a half-moon shape) then brush each side with olive oil.

**3** Place the folded, filled wraps onto the hot grill and cook for 3–5 minutes on each side until the cheese has melted and the wraps are golden and crisp.

**4** Remove from the grill and slice each cooked tortilla in half, to give you the classic 'quarter' quesadilla.

**HOT TIP**

Choose a vegan cheese that melts well, and experiment with the many varieties now available in supermarkets, including smoked and chilli flavours. I find that the cheese melts more evenly when grated just before using – note that pre-grated vegan cheeses are often coated with a starchy flour that keeps the strands separate in the packaging, but reduces the melt-ability.

# SMOKED SWEET POTATO CHILLI
## WITH CHOCOLATE AND CINNAMON

**BARBECUE COOKING TEMPERATURE:** high heat

**SERVES** 6

Barbecuing isn't just for summer – put a jumper on, heat up the grill for Halloween or Bonfire Night, and rustle up this smoky, sweet chilli that is made for sharing. Dark chocolate and a hint of cinnamon make for a rich and fragrant sauce, that has the perfect balance of warming flavours. Serve under the night sky, in warmed bowls, with coriander butter corn on the cob with lime (page 83), and cinder toffee (page 143) to finish.

1 x 400g (14oz) can of chopped tomatoes

1 onion, diced

1 green (bell) pepper, deseeded and diced

2 celery stalks, roughly chopped

1 rounded tsp mild chilli powder

1 tsp smoked paprika

½ tsp ground cinnamon

½ tsp dried oregano

1 square of dark chocolate (ensure dairy-free)

1 x 400g (14oz) can of red kidney beans, drained and rinsed

1 x 400g (14oz) can of black beans, drained and rinsed

1 large sweet potato, peeled and sliced into wedges

1 red (bell) pepper, deseeded and thickly sliced

1 tsp sunflower oil

generous pinch of sea salt

juice of ½ unwaxed lime

handful of fresh flat-leaf parsley, roughly torn

Pictured overleaf

**1** Add the chopped tomatoes, onion, green pepper, celery, chilli powder, paprika, cinnamon, oregano and chocolate to a 30cm (12in) carbon steel (barbecue safe) pan and place onto the hot grill. Cook for 5–10 minutes until bubbling, then stir in the kidney beans and black beans. Cook for a further 30–40 minutes, stirring frequently.

**2** Meanwhile, brush the sweet potato wedges and red pepper with sunflower oil. Carefully place the sweet potato wedges directly on the grill and cook for 25–30 minutes, turning a few times until softened. Add the red pepper to the grill when the barbecue is at a medium heat and cook for 10–12 minutes until softened.

**3** Remove the pan from the grill and stir in the sea salt and lime juice. Use tongs to lay the cooked sweet potato and pepper over the chilli, then scatter with flat-leaf parsley just before serving.

**HOT TIP**

This chilli can also be made on the hob. Cook the chilli in a large pan or cast-iron dish for around 25–30 minutes over a medium-high heat; grill the sweet potato in a griddle pan over a high heat for 15–20 minutes; and the red pepper for around 5–10 minutes until softened.

# PULLED MANGO TACOS
## WITH BEANS, RADISHES AND CORIANDER

**BARBECUE COOKING TEMPERATURE:**
medium heat

**SERVES** 4

Sweet, spiced mango becomes something special when grilled, which is why I make smoky pulled mango the star of the show in these family-friendly tacos. Personally, I love the contrast of the smooth mango in crunchy taco shells, but feel free to use soft corn wraps if you prefer. Serve with grilled guacamole (page 129).

1 x 400g (14oz) can of red kidney beans, drained and rinsed

3 spring onions (scallions), finely chopped

2 radishes, finely diced

3cm (1¼in) piece of cucumber, finely diced

handful of fresh coriander (cilantro) leaves, chopped

juice of ½ unwaxed lime

generous pinch of smoked sea salt

**For the pulled mango**

2 tbsp sunflower oil

1 tsp smoked paprika

pinch of mild chilli powder

pinch of sea salt

2 mangoes, peeled and sliced lengthways into 4 'cheeks' per mango

2 red (bell) peppers, deseeded and sliced into 8 thick strips

8 crunchy corn taco shells

2 tbsp vegan mayonnaise

**1** In a bowl, stir together the kidney beans, spring onions, radishes, cucumber, coriander and lime juice. Season to taste with smoked sea salt. Allow to infuse while you light the barbecue.

**2** In a bowl, whisk together the oil, smoked paprika, chilli powder and sea salt. Lay out the mango and peppers on a plate and brush both sides with the oil mix.

**3** Use tongs to place the mango and pepper slices onto the hot grill and cook for 5–6 minutes on each side until softened and sizzling and grill lines appear.

**4** Lay out the taco shells and spoon in the bean mix. Add the pepper slices.

**5** Place the mango onto a chopping board and use forks to gently pull the mango apart into finer shreds. Place into the taco shells and serve while still hot.

**HOT TIP**

These tacos are mildly spiced, making them perfect for younger eaters. If you prefer a little more heat, grill Padron peppers alongside the mango, or spoon over a few jalapeño pepper slices from the jar.

# SPICED YOGURT CAULIFLOWER
## AND MANGO

**BARBECUE COOKING TEMPERATURE:**
medium heat

**SERVES** 4

Marinate cauliflower florets in a simple spiced yogurt before barbecuing with mango, for an easy and delicious way to cook cauliflower that soaks up all the flavour you give it. Serve with mushroom masala sausages (page 64) and carrot, coriander and toasted cashew salad (page 114).

6 tbsp plain soya yogurt
1 tbsp sunflower oil
1 tbsp mild curry paste (ensure vegan)
½ tsp ground turmeric
½ tsp ground cumin
pinch of dried chilli flakes
pinch of sea salt
1 small cauliflower, leaves discarded, broken into about 16 bite-sized florets
2 firm mangoes, peeled and diced into about 12 bite-sized chunks
juice of ¼ unwaxed lemon
small handful of fresh coriander (cilantro) leaves, roughly torn

**1** In a large bowl, whisk together the yogurt, oil, curry paste, turmeric, cumin, chilli flakes and sea salt until combined.

**2** Add the cauliflower florets and coat in the marinade. Cover the bowl with cling film (plastic wrap) or a lid and allow to marinate for 2 hours.

**3** Shake off the excess yogurt marinade from the cauliflower florets and thread onto 4 metal skewers, alternating with the mango chunks. Aim for 4 cauliflower florets and 3 mango chunks per skewer.

**4** Place the skewers onto the hot grill and cook for 12–15 minutes, turning a few times to ensure even cooking. Remove from the grill and carefully slide the cauliflower and mango off the skewers. Squeeze over the lemon juice and scatter with coriander leaves.

### HOT TIP

As the mangoes cook on the barbecue, they soften and become sticky. Use slightly underripe mangoes so they thread firmly onto the skewer without breaking off during cooking.

# BUTTERED HASSELBACK SQUASH
## WITH CHIMICHURRI

**BARBECUE COOKING TEMPERATURE:**
medium heat. Move some of the charcoal to the side so part of the grill has indirect heat.

**SERVES** 4

Buttery, bay-infused butternut squash becomes the star of the show when barbecued, with the sweet flavour balanced by fresh chimichurri. A sharp, Y-shaped vegetable peeler will take the skin off the butternut squash with ease: peel off the whiteish area under the skin too, to reveal the firm orange flesh. Perfect with charred pepper orzo salad with olives (page 106) and sage and onion sausage rolls with ketchup (page 102).

1 medium butternut squash, peeled and halved lengthways, seeds discarded
3 tbsp vegan butter
1 dried bay leaf
generous pinch of sea salt and black pepper

For the chimichurri
30g (1oz) fresh flat-leaf parsley, finely chopped
½ tsp dried oregano
½ tsp smoked paprika
pinch of dried chilli flakes
juice of 1 unwaxed lemon
2 tsp cider vinegar
150ml (generous ½ cup) extra virgin olive oil

Also pictured on pages 110–111

**1** Place half of the butternut squash onto a chopping board, flat-side down so it doesn't wobble. Carefully slice into the squash widthways, cutting a slice every 5mm (¼in). Be careful not to cut all the way down to the chopping board (see 'Hot Tip'). Repeat with the remaining half.

**2** In a small pan, heat the butter and bay leaf over a low heat until melted. Allow to stand for a moment, then discard the bay leaf. Brush the butternut squash with the melted butter, pushing it into the slices too. Sprinkle over the salt and pepper.

**3** Place onto the grill over the area of indirect heat. Place the lid down or loosely cover with foil and cook for 45 minutes, rotating a couple of times. Remove the lid or foil and cook for a further 15 minutes, or until tender.

**4** Meanwhile, make the chimichurri by tossing the chopped parsley, oregano, paprika and chilli flakes into a bowl. Stir in the lemon juice, cider vinegar and olive oil and mix until evenly distributed. Season to taste with salt and pepper, then allow to stand and infuse.

**5** Carefully remove the cooked squash from the barbecue and place onto a serving plate. Generously spoon over the chimichurri.

**HOT TIP**

For the perfect hasselback effect, place chopsticks or spoons lengthways, at either side of the squash, before you start slicing through the flesh. This will prevent the knife from cutting too far into the squash.

# MEDITERRANEAN SAUSAGES

**BARBECUE COOKING
TEMPERATURE:**
low-medium heat

**MAKES** 8

Bite into a taste of the Mediterranean with these homemade sausages packed with red pepper, tomatoes, spinach and mushrooms. They are full of flavour and colour and are so grill-able – perfect for any barbecue – resulting in a crisp outer and tender middle. Serve with barbecue patatas bravas (page 86) and a jug of sangria (page 148).

1 tbsp sunflower oil, plus
   1 tbsp for brushing
200g (7oz) chestnut
   mushrooms, brushed
   clean and roughly sliced
1 red (bell) pepper, deseeded
   and roughly chopped
4 cherry tomatoes
generous handful of fresh
   spinach leaves
½ tsp dried oregano
1 garlic clove, crushed
6 rounded tbsp rolled oats
generous pinch of sea salt
   and black pepper
4 rice paper wraps

**1** Heat the oil in a large pan over a medium heat on the hob. Add the mushrooms and pepper and cook for 5–6 minutes until they begin to soften. Add the tomatoes and spinach and cook for a further 5 minutes. Stir in the oregano and garlic and cook for a further minute until fragrant.

**2** Allow the vegetables to cool a little, then transfer to a high-powered jug blender or food processor. Stir in the oats with a generous pinch of salt and black pepper. Blitz until semi-smooth and combined, then spoon into a bowl and cover with cling film (plastic wrap) or secure a clean cloth over the top. Refrigerate overnight, or for at least 6 hours.

**3** Fill a large bowl with warm (not hot) water. Brush a clean worksurface or board with a little sunflower oil, as well as a plate to hold the sausages before you barbecue them. Dip a rice paper wrap into the water

for 3–5 seconds until it begins to soften. Remove from the water and place on the oiled worksurface or board. Use a knife to slice the rice paper wrap in half.

**4** Spoon 1 tablespoon of the chilled sausage mixture onto the middle of each half, spreading it down the length in a sausage shape. Roll the sides of the wraps in, then fold or twist the ends in to make a sausage shape. Place on the oiled plate while you prepare the other sausages with softened rice paper wraps.

**5** Brush the sausages with a little oil, then carefully place on the grill. Cook for 10–12 minutes, turning every few minutes to ensure even cooking and a crispy skin.

**HOT TIP**

Rice paper wraps can be found in supermarkets, and are simple and versatile to use with a little practice. See page 64 for tips on using rice paper wraps.

# STONE-BAKED PIZZAS

**BARBECUE COOKING TEMPERATURE:** high heat

**SERVES** 2

Nothing beats the crisp but fluffy bite of a stone-baked pizza. They are so easy to make using the high heat from your barbecue, simply by using a pizza stone. This is a recipe for a simple vegan margherita pizza, but feel free to add the toppings of your choice. Choose a vegan hard cheese that melts well, or switch to a classic Italian pizza rosso, which has no cheese but plenty of sauce, herbs and veggie toppings.

### For the pizza sauce

1 tbsp olive oil

2 garlic cloves, crushed

250g (9oz) good-quality passata (sieved tomatoes)

pinch of sugar

handful of fresh basil leaves, finely chopped

¼ tsp dried oregano

generous pinch of sea salt and black pepper

### For the base

300g (2¼ cups) strong white bread flour or '00' flour, plus extra for kneading

7g (¼oz) sachet of fast-action dried yeast

pinch of sugar

1 tsp salt

1 tbsp olive oil

2 tbsp semolina flour, for dusting

### For the toppings

1 beef tomato, thinly sliced into half-rounds

200g (7oz) vegan hard cheese, grated

handful of fresh basil leaves

drizzle of extra virgin olive oil

pinch of sea salt and black pepper

**1** To make the pizza sauce, add the oil and garlic to a pan and heat over a medium heat on the hob for 2–3 minutes until fragrant. Stir in the passata and sugar, then cook for 5 minutes, stirring often. Remove from the heat and stir in the basil leaves, oregano, salt and plenty of pepper. Set aside. (This can be made up to 2 days in advance and kept in the fridge in a sealed container.)

**2** To make the base, add the flour, yeast, sugar and salt to a bowl and stir to combine. Stir in the olive oil with 200ml (generous ¾ cup) warm water and bring together to form a dough.

**3** Dust a clean, flat surface with a little flour, then knead the dough for 5 minutes. Halve the dough and place the bowl over it to prove for 15 minutes. Remove the bowl and dust a clean flat surface with semolina flour (1 tablespoon for each base). Roll each ball of dough to roughly 30cm (12in) in diameter using a rolling pin.

**4** Carefully place the pizza stone on the hot grill, close the lid and heat for 15 minutes.

**5** If you have a pizza peel, go ahead and lay a pizza base onto the peel, then top with the sauce, sliced tomato and grated cheese. If you don't have a pizza peel, you may find it easier to slide the pizza base onto the hot pizza stone first (the semolina flour will help with this), and then add the sauce, sliced tomato and grated cheese when the base is in position on the stone.

**6** Cook the pizza for 7–8 minutes until the edges begin to brown, then close the barbecue lid to help the cheese melt. This should take 2–3 minutes.

**7** Remove the pizza from the stone and top with fresh basil leaves and a drizzle of extra virgin olive oil. Season to taste with salt and pepper.

# CRISPY BALSAMIC GNOCCHI
## WITH SWEET PEPPERS AND TOMATOES

**BARBECUE COOKING TEMPERATURE:**
medium heat

**SERVES** 4 generously

Barbecued potato gnocchi is unexpectedly crispy and delicious, especially when brushed with a quick balsamic reduction and served with grilled peppers and tomatoes. Brush the grill with a little olive oil while the coals are coming up to temperature to avoid the gnocchi sticking, and allow it to crisp up for a few minutes before turning the skewers.

100ml (scant ½ cup) balsamic vinegar

2 tsp granulated sugar

1 tbsp olive oil

500g (1lb 2oz) shop-bought potato gnocchi (ensure vegan) (see Hot Tip)

2 red (bell) peppers, deseeded and chopped into chunky pieces

16 cherry tomatoes

**1** Add the balsamic vinegar and sugar to a small pan and bring to the boil over a medium heat on the hob. Simmer for 5 minutes, then remove from the heat (it will thicken slightly as it cools).

**2** Place the gnocchi into a large, heatproof bowl and pour over enough just-boiled water to cover. Allow to stand for 3–5 minutes, then rinse. Dry with kitchen paper or a clean tea towel to remove as much surface liquid as possible.

**3** Thread the gnocchi onto 4 or 6 metal skewers, alternating with chunks of pepper and tomatoes. (I usually add 2–3 gnocchi, then one piece of pepper, 2–3 gnocchi, then one tomato, until the skewers are full). Brush the gnocchi, peppers and tomatoes with olive oil, then generously brush the gnocchi with the cooled balsamic reduction.

**4** Place the skewers onto the hot grill and cook for 4–5 minutes, then turn and cook for a further 4–5 minutes. Cook for a further couple of minutes to really crisp up the gnocchi.

**5** Remove from the grill and carefully slide the gnocchi, peppers and tomatoes onto plates. Serve hot.

### HOT TIP

Shop-bought potato gnocchi is an essential for any store cupboard for a quick and speedy supper, or tasty addition to a barbecue! Many supermarket own-brands do not contain egg or animal products, but always check the ingredients before purchasing.

# HERBY MEATBALLS
## IN ARRABBIATA SAUCE

**BARBECUE COOKING TEMPERATURE:** high heat

**SERVES** 2

Vegan meatballs are a real crowd-pleaser, especially when they've absorbed the smoky flavours from the barbecue, and are served in a fiery arrabbiata sauce. Prepare the meatballs in advance and allow them to rest and firm up in the fridge for a fail-safe recipe that can easily be doubled up. Serve with cooked pasta, or in a warmed bread bun for a sub-style sandwich.

### For the herby meatballs

1 x 400g (14oz) can of black beans, drained and rinsed

2 tbsp walnuts

2 rounded tbsp rolled oats

1 tsp dried mixed herbs

½ tsp dried sage

generous pinch of sea salt and black pepper

1 tbsp olive oil

### For the arrabbiata sauce

2 garlic cloves, crushed

generous pinch of dried chilli flakes

300g (10oz) good-quality passata (sieved tomatoes)

pinch of granulated sugar

pinch of sea salt and black pepper

handful of fresh flat-leaf parsley, finely chopped

**1** Dry the rinsed black beans on kitchen paper or with a clean cloth. Add the black beans to a high-powered blender jug along with the walnuts, oats, mixed herbs, sage, salt and black pepper. Pulse until semi-smooth, scraping the mixture down a few times with a spatula (leave a few chunks remaining for texture)

**2** Roll into 8 meatballs, using approximately 2 rounded teaspoons of the mixture per meatball. Place onto a plate and cover with cling film (plastic wrap). Refrigerate for at least 6 hours, or overnight.

**3** Add the olive oil to a 30cm (12in) carbon steel (barbecue safe) pan and place on the grill until the oil is hot. Carefully add the meatballs and cook for 10–12 minutes, rotating and turning once each side is browned.

**4** Add the garlic and chilli flakes to the pan for a minute, stirring constantly. Pour the passata into the pan, surrounding the meatballs but not covering them – the sauce may splatter a little, so be sure to wear an apron! Stir in the sugar and cook for 3–5 minutes.

**5** Remove the pan from the grill and season with salt and pepper. Scatter over the flat-leaf parsley and serve hot.

### HOT TIP

To save time at the grill side, make up the arrabbiata sauce on the hob in advance (adding in a drizzle of olive oil to cook the garlic and chilli flakes). This sauce will keep in the fridge for up to 4 days in a sealed container and is suitable for freezing.

# NO-LOBSTER ROLLS

**BARBECUE COOKING TEMPERATURE:**
high-medium heat. Move some of the charcoal to the side so part of the grill has indirect heat.

**SERVES** 4

New England-style lobster rolls are veganized with tender jackfruit along with all the familiar additions, including lemon juice, mayonnaise and diced celery. Jackfruit absorbs the delicate flavours of lemon butter, but stands up to the smokiness of the barbecue (and cooking it on the barbecue really transforms the flavour). I love to serve the filling warm, loaded into toasted hot dog buns, with cool mayonnaise and crisp iceberg lettuce.

2 tbsp vegan butter
zest of 1 unwaxed lemon, finely grated
1 x 400g (14oz) can of jackfruit, drained and rinsed, broken into small pieces
4 radishes, finely chopped into half-rounds
1 celery stalk, finely diced
3 rounded tbsp vegan mayonnaise
small handful of fresh dill, finely chopped
small handful of fresh chives, finely chopped
squeeze of juice from 1 unwaxed lemon
pinch of sea salt
4 hot dog buns
¼ iceberg lettuce, shredded
few pinches of paprika

**1** Place a 30cm (12in) carbon steel (barbecue safe) pan over the area of indirect heat and gently melt the butter for a few minutes. Add the lemon zest and stir until fragrant.

**2** Dry the rinsed jackfruit on kitchen paper or a clean cloth. Add the chunks to the pan and cook for 5–10 minutes, stirring frequently, until the lemony butter is absorbed and the jackfruit is hot.

**3** Remove the pan from the heat and stir in the radishes, celery, vegan mayonnaise, dill and chives. Squeeze in a little lemon juice and season to taste with sea salt.

**4** Split or pull open the bread buns and toast on the grill until charred. Load the shredded lettuce and the jackfruit mix into the toasted bread buns, finish with a pinch of paprika and serve warm.

**HOT TIP**

Mix together the radishes, celery, mayonnaise, dill and chives in a bowl up to a day in advance, for a quicker dish at the grill side.

# SIZZLING FAJITAS
## WITH CHARRED LIME

**BARBECUE COOKING TEMPERATURE:**
medium-high heat

**SERVES** 4

I'm a convert to firing up the barbecue just to cook fajitas (and a couple of sides), as the smoky, charred flavour can't be matched with pans and grills in the kitchen. Meaty chestnut mushrooms, peppers and red onion are basted in spices, barbecued until sizzling, then served in warm wraps. Top with quick pink pickles (page 125) and wedges of the charred lime for squeezing.

1 tsp mild chilli powder
1 tsp smoked paprika
½ tsp dried oregano
¼ tsp ground cinnamon
1 tsp sea salt
1 rounded tbsp tomato ketchup
3 tbsp sunflower oil
12 chestnut mushrooms, brushed clean
1 yellow (bell) pepper, sliced into thick strips
1 red (bell) pepper, deseeded and sliced into thick strips
1 large red onion, deseeded and sliced into wedges
1 unwaxed lime, quartered
4 large tortilla wraps
½ iceberg lettuce, shredded
handful of fresh coriander (cilantro), roughly torn

**1** In a bowl, stir together the chilli powder, smoked paprika, oregano, cinnamon and sea salt. Stir in the ketchup and oil until combined. Allow to infuse for a few minutes.

**2** Thread the mushrooms, peppers and onion onto 4 skewers (aiming for 3 mushrooms, 3–4 strips of peppers and 3–4 wedges of red onion per skewer). Brush liberally with the spiced oil mix, ensuring all surfaces of the vegetables are coated.

**3** Place the skewers onto the hot grill and cook for 10–12 minutes, turning frequently to ensure even cooking. Baste with any remaining spiced oil mix.

**4** Add the lime wedges to the grill and cook for 3–4 minutes until charred, turning once.

**5** Remove the skewers from the grill and allow them to rest for a couple of minutes. Meanwhile, throw the tortilla wraps onto the grill for a few seconds to warm until grill marks appear.

**6** Place the wraps on serving plates and lay on some shredded lettuce. Carefully remove the vegetables from the skewers and add to the wraps (one skewer of sizzling vegetable per wrap). Squeeze over some charred lime and top with coriander and quick pink pickles.

**HOT TIP**

Threading the vegetables onto skewers is a quicker way to cook the fajitas, as you won't have to individually turn each vegetable with tongs; simply turn the skewer and they will all cook and turn together.

# PEANUT BUTTER AND CHILLI JAM BEAN BURGERS
## WITH PRETZELS

**BARBECUE COOKING TEMPERATURE:**
medium heat

**SERVES** 6

A good bean burger is hard to find: they are either too complicated to make, don't hold together well, or lack a certain something. This recipe has been a fail-safe favourite of mine for years on the barbecue (and beyond) with bite, texture and plenty of flavour to stand up to the smokiness. It's gently spiced and flavoured with rich peanut butter, then glazed with sticky chilli jam that mellows as it caramelizes. Finish off with salted pretzels in a toasted bun. Prepare in advance and refrigerate overnight to allow the burgers to come together. A party-pleasing burger that everyone will love.

1 x 400g (14oz) can of black beans, drained and rinsed

1 x 400g (14oz) can of red kidney beans, drained and rinsed

4 tbsp rolled oats

4 spring onions (scallions), finely chopped

2 tbsp smooth peanut butter

½ tsp mild chilli powder

½ tsp smoked paprika

pinch of ground cinnamon

small handful of fresh coriander (cilantro) leaves, torn

pinch of sea salt and black pepper

2 tbsp sunflower oil

2 tbsp chilli jam

6 burger buns

6 leaves of iceberg lettuce

1 beef tomato, thinly sliced

about 18 salted pretzels

Pictured overleaf and on pages 18 and 25

**1** Pat dry the rinsed black beans and kidney beans with kitchen paper or a clean towel, then tip into a blender jug or food processor, with the oats, spring onions, peanut butter, chilli powder, paprika, cinnamon, coriander, salt and pepper. Pulse a few times until you have a semi-smooth mixture (you may have to scrape the mixture down with a spatula) leaving a few beans chunky for texture.

**2** Shape into burger patties using 2 tablespoons of the mixture per burger, or press into a burger shaper to a thickness of 2.5–3cm (1–1¼in). Place the six burger patties onto a plate and cover with cling film (plastic wrap). Refrigerate overnight, or for at least 6 hours.

**3** Remove the burger patties from the fridge and brush over all surfaces with 1 tablespoon of the oil. Place the burgers onto the hot grill and cook for 4–5 minutes until crisp and browned before carefully flipping over. A flat spatula is often easier than tongs for this job.

**4** In a small bowl, mix the remaining oil and with the chilli jam. When both sides of the burgers are browned, brush over the oil and chilli jam mix and cook for a further minute on each side.

**5** Lightly toast the burger buns and add the lettuce and tomato slices. Top with the burgers and lay 3 pretzels over the top of each burger. Enjoy hot.

**HOT TIP**

Allow the burgers to cook until crisp and firm for about 4–5 minutes before flipping to prevent any breakage.

# PIZZA-STUFFED MUSHROOMS
## WITH CRISPY CROÛTONS

**BARBECUE COOKING TEMPERATURE:**
medium heat

**SERVES** 4

These juicy, meaty mushrooms are loaded with pizza toppings and crunchy croûtons – a light and fun addition to your barbecue! The smokiness of a barbecue infuses the mushrooms with flavour that just can't be matched in the oven. Feel free to add a handful of grated vegan cheese, if you like.

4 large flat mushrooms, peeled and inner stalk removed

1 tbsp olive oil

4 tbsp tomato purée (paste)

generous pinch of dried oregano

½ yellow (bell) pepper, deseeded and diced

4 pitted green olives, sliced

2 cherry tomatoes, halved

generous pinch of sea salt and black pepper

8 croûtons

handful of wild rocket (arugula)

**1** Brush the outside areas of the mushrooms with olive oil.

**2** Spoon the tomato purée into the middle cavity of the mushrooms and spread it out, then sprinkle with dried oregano. Add the yellow pepper, olives and tomatoes and season with a pinch of salt and pepper.

**3** Place the mushrooms onto the hot grill, toppings-side up. Cook for 5 minutes, then close the lid on the barbecue (or loosely cover with foil if your barbecue doesn't have a lid) and cook for a further 5 minutes to soften the toppings.

**4** Remove from the grill and press in a couple of croûtons per mushroom. Top with rocket and serve hot.

**HOT TIP**

Shop-bought croûtons work well in this recipe, or simply make your own by cutting a thick slice of white bread into chunks, and throwing into a roasting tray with 1 tablespoon olive oil and a pinch of salt. Cook in a preheated oven at 180°C/350°F/gas mark 4 for 8–10 minutes until golden and crisp.

# SQUASH, APPLE AND CHESTNUT MUSHROOM SKEWERS
## WITH THYME OIL

**BARBECUE COOKING TEMPERATURE:**
medium heat

**SERVES** 4

Work this wonderful flavour combination into a rustic-style barbecue, for a dish that delivers on satisfaction every time. Chestnut mushrooms have a nutty depth of flavour that other small mushrooms just don't deliver on, as well as a meaty texture when barbecued. Perfect for late summer barbecues, although I've been known to fire up the barbecue on a dry autumn day to cook these fall-flavoured skewers!

2 rounded tbsp olive oil

2 sprigs of fresh thyme

1 butternut squash, peeled and chopped into bite-sized chunks

12 chestnut mushrooms, brushed clean

2 red apples, chopped into bite-sized chunks

pinch of sea salt and black pepper

**1** Spoon the oil into a small bowl. Remove the thyme leaves from the sprigs and stir them into the oil. Allow to infuse for 10–15 minutes.

**2** Thread the chunks of butternut squash, mushrooms and apple onto metal skewers, aiming for around 4 pieces of butternut squash, 3 chunks of apple and 3 chestnut mushrooms per skewer. Brush generously with the thyme-infused oil.

**3** Place the skewers onto the grill and cook for 15–20 minutes, basting with the oil as needed. Turn frequently until the squash has softened and the mushrooms and apples have lightly browned in places.

**4** Carefully remove from the grill and season with salt and pepper. Serve on the skewers for guests to remove onto their own plates.

**HOT TIP**

It is easier to thread the butternut squash and apple onto metal skewers rather than soaked wooden skewers, which are prone to snapping.

# CARIBBEAN CAULIFLOWER
## WITH PINEAPPLE AND BLACK BEAN SALSA

**BARBECUE COOKING TEMPERATURE:**
medium heat

**SERVES** 4

These cauliflower steaks are marinated in a fragrant, spiced yogurt before being grilled on the barbecue until tender.
Top with a zingy, fruity salsa and black beans for a dish that's fresh, fun and tastes like holidays. Delicious with simple salt-baked potatoes (page 82).

4 rounded tbsp coconut yogurt
1 tsp jerk seasoning
½ tsp smoked paprika
½ tsp ground cinnamon
½ tsp mild chilli powder
pinch of black pepper
2 tbsp sunflower oil
2 large cauliflowers, outer leaves discarded

**For the pineapple and black bean salsa**

1 x 400g (14oz) can of black beans, drained and rinsed
½ small fresh pineapple, peeled and diced
4cm (1½in) piece of cucumber, diced
2 spring onions (scallions), finely chopped
handful of fresh coriander (cilantro), finely chopped
juice of ½ unwaxed lime
pinch of sea salt

**1** In a large bowl, stir together the coconut yogurt, jerk seasoning, smoked paprika, cinnamon, chilli powder and black pepper. Whisk in the sunflower oil and set aside.

**2** Place a whole cauliflower on a chopping board and slice two 'steaks' lengthways from the middle core of the cauliflower. Use the base as a guide for where this firm area sits. (See Hot Tip for ways to use the remaining florets.) Dip the cauliflower steaks into the spiced yogurt to coat and allow to marinate for 1–2 hours.

**3** Meanwhile make the salsa. In a bowl, stir together the black beans, pineapple, cucumber, spring onions and coriander. Squeeze in the lime juice and season to taste with salt. Set aside.

**4** Shake the cauliflower steaks gently to remove the excess yogurt and place them onto the hot grill. Cook for 8–10 minutes on each side until golden and tender.

**5** Transfer to plates and serve with the salsa generously spooned over the cauliflower steaks.

**HOT TIP**

This recipe requires the firm 'steaks' from the middle of the cauliflower, so reserve the cauliflower florets for another recipe, such as spiced yogurt cauliflower and mango (page 44), throw into a summery coconut milk curry, or bake in the oven with barbecue sauce for cauliflower wings!

# GRILL-SIDE KATSU BURGER
## WITH WASABI MAYO

**BARBECUE COOKING TEMPERATURE:**
medium-high heat

**SERVES** 2

Bring your favourite Japanese-style dish to the barbecue, with this tender and crisp tofu burger. The smooth katsu sauce coats the grilled tofu, before it is tossed in golden, crisp panko breadcrumbs. Some of this recipe is pre-cooked on the hob, some of it is grilled on the barbecue, but it is assembled at the grill side for a speedy and satisfying burger when you're ready to eat it. Serve with plenty of quick pink pickles (page 125) and a wedge of charred lime, if you like.

### For the katsu sauce
1 tbsp sunflower oil
1 onion, roughly chopped
1 carrot, peeled and roughly chopped
2cm (¾in) piece of ginger, peeled and roughly chopped
2 garlic cloves, sliced
1 tbsp mild curry powder
1 x 400ml (14fl oz) can of full-fat coconut milk
2 tsp maple syrup
2 tsp soy sauce
1 tsp cornflour (cornstarch)

### For the wasabi mayo
1 tbsp vegan mayonnaise
1 tsp wasabi paste

### For the burgers
6 tbsp panko breadcrumbs
280g (9oz) block of pre-pressed extra-firm tofu (see page 20), blotted of excess moisture, sliced horizontally into 2 pieces
1 tbsp sunflower oil
2 sesame topped burger buns (ensure vegan)

Also pictured on pages 122–123

**1** Start by making the katsu sauce. Heat the oil, onion and carrot in a pan over a medium heat on the hob for 3–4 minutes until they begin to soften. Add the ginger, garlic and curry powder and cook for a further 2 minutes. Pour in the coconut milk, maple syrup and soy sauce, then cook for 15 minutes.

**2** Ladle or pour into a high-powered jug blender and blitz until completely smooth. Pour the sauce back into the pan. Mix the cornflour with 2 tablespoons water, then whisk and cook over a medium heat for 10 minutes until thickened and smooth. Set aside in a large bowl.

**3** Next prepare the wasabi mayo. In a bowl, whisk together the vegan mayonnaise and wasabi paste until combined. Set aside.

**4** Add the panko breadcrumbs to a dry pan on the hob and toast for 2–3 minutes, or until lightly golden, tossing frequently to avoid burning. Encourage even toasting by having a flat layer of breadcrumbs in the pan. Remove from the heat when lightly golden and set aside on a plate.

**5** Brush the tofu pieces with oil. Place on the hot grill for 4–5 minutes, then flip to cook the other side until golden and firm.

**6** Remove the cooked tofu from the grill and dip into the katsu sauce, covering all areas. Shake off any excess, then press the coated tofu into the golden panko breadcrumbs. Carefully place back onto the grill for up to 30 seconds to heat through.

**7** Lightly toast the bread buns for a few seconds, then place the burgers inside them. Spoon in the wasabi mayo and top with quick pink pickles (page 125).

# MUSHROOM MASALA SAUSAGES

**BARBECUE COOKING TEMPERATURE:**
low-medium heat

**MAKES** 6

These sausages have a crispy outer skin and a meaty mushroom filling flavoured with delicate spices, and are finished with a smoky hit from the barbecue. The sausages can be made a few hours in advance, then stored on a lightly oiled plate to avoid sticking. Delicious served with garlic naan breads (page 94), and a spoonful of mango chutney.

1 tbsp sunflower oil, plus 1 tbsp for brushing

250g (9oz) chestnut mushrooms, brushed clean and roughly chopped

1 tsp mustard seeds

½ tsp ground cumin

½ tsp dried chilli flakes

2 garlic cloves, crushed

2 spring onions (scallions), finely chopped

generous handful of fresh coriander (cilantro) leaves

6 tbsp rolled oats

generous pinch of sea salt and black pepper

3 rice paper wraps

**1** Heat the oil in a large pan over a medium-high heat on the hob and throw in the mushrooms. Cook for 3–4 minutes until fragrant, then add the mustard seeds, cumin, chilli flakes, garlic and spring onions and cook for a further 2 minutes, stirring frequently to avoid sticking. Remove from the heat and stir in the coriander.

**2** Add the oats to a high-powered jug blender and blitz for a few seconds until they become finer. Add the cooked mushroom mix and season with salt and plenty of pepper, then blitz again until thick and coarse.

**3** Fill a large bowl with warm (not hot) water. Brush a clean worksurface or board with a little sunflower oil, as well as a plate to hold the sausages before you barbecue them. Dip a rice paper wrap into the water for 3–5 seconds until it begins to soften. Remove from the water and place on the oiled worksurface or board. Use a knife to slice the rice paper wrap in half.

**4** Spoon 1 tablespoon of the blitzed mushroom mixture onto the middle of each half, spreading it down the length in a sausage shape. Roll the sides of the wraps in, then fold or twist the ends. Place on the oiled plate while you prepare the other 4 sausages with softened rice paper wraps.

**5** Brush the sausages with a little oil, then carefully place on the grill. Cook for 12–15 minutes, turning every few minutes to ensure even cooking and a crispy skin.

## HOT TIP

Rice paper wraps can be found in the world aisle of large supermarkets. They may be called Vietnamese spring roll wraps, but are not to be confused with the crispy wraps used to make Chinese-style spring rolls. Some brands of rice paper wraps are made from tapioca flour, making them translucent, which is perfect for casing vegan sausages.

# COOLING-COALS MOUSSAKA

**BARBECUE COOKING TEMPERATURE:** low heat

**SERVES** 4

Make the most of the residual heat from the barbecue, and grill aubergine slices as the coals are cooling, ready to layer into a moussaka. Aubergine takes on a wonderful smoky flavour on a charcoal barbecue, which simply can't be replicated on a griddle pan. Layer with a rich tomato and lentil mince, and nutmeg-infused yogurt. Serve with crusty bread, vegan butter and green salad.

2 aubergines (eggplants), thinly sliced lengthways
1 tbsp olive oil

**For the tomato lentil mince**
1 tbsp olive oil
1 onion, diced
3 garlic cloves, crushed
1 tsp dried oregano
1 tsp paprika
½ tsp ground cinnamon
1 x 400g (14oz) can of good-quality chopped tomatoes
1 x 400g (14oz) can of green lentils, drained and rinsed
generous pinch of sea salt and black pepper
handful of fresh flat-leaf parsley, roughly chopped

**For the yogurt sauce**
8 tbsp plain soya yogurt
pinch of grated nutmeg
pinch of sea salt

**1** Lay the aubergines onto a plate and brush both sides with olive oil. Place in an even layer onto the barbecue grill, as the coals are beginning to cool down. Cook until golden with char lines on each side, for about 8–15 minutes (depending on how cool the barbecue is at this point). Remove from the grill and set aside.

**2** In a pan on the hob, heat the oil and onion over a medium-high heat for 2–3 minutes until the onion begins to soften. Add the garlic, oregano, paprika and cinnamon and cook for a further minute, stirring constantly to avoid burning.

**3** Pour in the chopped tomatoes and green lentils, reduce the heat to medium, then simmer for 15 minutes, stirring occasionally. Season to taste with salt and pepper and stir in the flat-leaf parsley.

**4** Preheat the oven to 180°C/350°F/gas mark 4. Meanwhile, spoon the yogurt, nutmeg and sea salt into a bowl and stir until combined.

**5** Layer the cooked aubergine, tomato lentil mince and yogurt sauce into a deep baking dish (aim for 4–5 layers) then bake in the oven for 30–35 minutes until bubbling.

**HOT TIP**

If you don't want to cook up the moussaka on the same day, the aubergine slices will keep for up to 2 days in the fridge when drizzled with a little extra olive oil.

# GRILLED WATERMELON
## WITH THAI GREEN CURRY

**BARBECUE COOKING TEMPERATURE:** high heat

**SERVES** 4

If you've never barbecued watermelon before, prepare for succulent meatiness that you wouldn't expect to come from the fruit – the transformation is incredible. It looks (and tastes) wonderful over the creamy coconut curry, too. I love cooking up a curry outdoors, it is as enjoyable to cook as it is to eat! Serve with nutty rice salad (page 117) and sticky broccoli with soy, chilli and sesame (page 79).

1 tbsp sunflower oil, plus
   1 tbsp for brushing

2 spring onions (scallions),
   finely diced

2 garlic cloves, crushed

1 red chilli, deseeded and
   thinly sliced

8 stems of Tenderstem
   broccoli

8 stems of asparagus,
   tough ends discarded

8 sugarsnap peas, halved
   lengthways

4 baby corns, halved
   lengthways

4 tbsp frozen or fresh
   edamame beans

1 rounded tbsp Thai green
   curry paste (ensure vegan)

1 x 400g (14oz) can of full-fat
   coconut milk

1 tbsp soy sauce

½ watermelon, sliced into
   3 wedges, flesh sliced into
   1cm (½in) thick triangles

2 unwaxed limes, halved

pinch of sea salt

handful of salted peanuts,
   roughly chopped

handful of fresh coriander
   (cilantro) leaves, torn

**1** Add 1 tablespoon oil to a 30cm (12in) carbon steel pan (barbecue safe) and place onto the grill. When the oil is hot, add the spring onions, garlic and chilli and cook for 1–2 minutes until fragrant.

**2** Add the broccoli, asparagus, sugarsnap peas and baby corns and cook for 2–3 minutes, stirring frequently until coated in the fragrant oil.

**3** Add the edamame beans and Thai green curry paste and stir. Pour in the coconut milk, then cook for 15–20 minutes until the vegetables have softened. Stir in the soy sauce.

**4** Meanwhile, brush the watermelon with a little oil and place onto the grill. Cook for 4–5 minutes until tender and grill lines appear, then use tongs to turn and cook for a further 4–5 minutes. Place the limes onto the grill, cut-side down, and char for 3–5 minutes.

**5** Sprinkle the watermelon and lime with a pinch of sea salt. Lay the cooked watermelon over the curry. Scatter over the peanuts and coriander, and serve with the charred lime for squeezing.

**HOT TIP**

The Thai green curry is simple and easy to cook on the barbecue, just have all the ingredients prepared and at hand for ease. The curry can also be made in advance on the hob, before being topped with the barbecued watermelon.

# SIZZLING SIDES

# FIRE-ROASTED TOMATO GAZPACHO

**BARBECUE COOKING TEMPERATURE:**
medium heat

**SERVES** 4

Perfect for a summer lunch or as an *amuse bouche*, this smooth and chilled soup has a wonderful depth of flavour from the charred tomatoes. It works best when a few different varieties of ripe tomatoes are used to create a rich and jammy flavour. Allow the gazpacho to chill for a least 1 hour, longer is better, to allow the flavours to mingle and intensify. Serve chilled in small glasses

600g (1lb 5oz) mixed size and colour tomatoes
1 tbsp olive oil, plus extra for drizzling
¼ cucumber, roughly chopped
1 tsp cider vinegar
pinch of caster (superfine) sugar
pinch of mixed spice
generous pinch of sea salt and black pepper
handful of small fresh basil leaves

**1** Thread any small tomatoes onto skewers and halve the larger tomatoes. Brush the tomatoes with olive oil.

**2** Place the skewers and tomato halves (cut-side down) onto the grill. Cook for 10–15 minutes until blistered and jammy with some areas of charring, turning the skewers and tomato halves every few minutes.

**3** Remove the tomatoes from the grill. Add them to a high-powered jug blender, along with the cucumber, cider vinegar, caster sugar, mixed spice, salt and pepper. Blitz until smooth.

**4** Taste the gazpacho and add extra salt and pepper to taste.

**5** Refrigerate for at least 1 hour. Top with small leaves of basil and drizzle over a little olive oil just before serving.

**HOT TIP**

Add an alternative crunchy topping of diced celery, flaked (slivered) almonds and flat-leaf parsley, if you like.

# MARINATED ANTIPASTI

**BARBECUE COOKING TEMPERATURE:**
medium-high heat

**SERVES** 6

Make the most of seasonal summer produce by creating your own vegetable antipasti. It's simple to make and showcases the vegetables wonderfully, so use good-quality olive oil for extra fruitiness. Serve with warmed breads, olives and balsamic vinegar, or over salt-baked potatoes (page 82), or spoon into clean jars and gift to friends and family.

6 tbsp good-quality olive oil, plus extra for drizzling

2 sprigs of fresh thyme, leaves picked

pinch of dried mixed herbs

½ tsp sea salt

generous pinch of black pepper

1 red (bell) pepper, deseeded and quartered

1 green (bell) pepper, deseeded and quartered

1 yellow (bell) pepper, deseeded and quartered

1 courgette (zucchini), roughly sliced lengthways

200g (7oz) vine tomatoes, left on the vine

1 tbsp cider vinegar

2 garlic cloves, smashed

**1** In a large bowl, mix together the 6 tablespoons olive oil, the thyme leaves, mixed herbs, salt and pepper. Brush all the vegetables with some of the herby oil, leaving the remaining oil in the bowl.

**2** Place all of the peppers, the courgette and tomatoes onto the hot grill and cook for 3–5 minutes on each side until charred and softened.

**3** Once cooked, place the vegetables back into the oil mix in the bowl. Drizzle over a little extra olive oil and stir in the cider vinegar and garlic cloves. Allow to stand for at least 1 hour for the most tender antipasti.

**HOT TIP**

Grilling the vegetables on the barbecue infuses them with an unbeatable smoky flavour, but to prepare them in advance without lighting the barbecue, use a griddle pan on the hob to cook the vegetables until charred lines appear on both sides and the vegetables have softened.

# HERITAGE TOMATO BRUSCHETTA

**BARBECUE COOKING
TEMPERATURE:** high heat

**SERVES** 4

Tomato bruschetta is the taste of summer, with tangy sweet heritage tomatoes, basil, and lightly charred crusty bread. Serve as an appetizer with a sparkling, citrus aperitif for a simple, wholesome way to start your barbecue.

200g (7oz) mixed baby tomatoes, roughly quartered

generous handful of fresh basil leaves, roughly chopped

2 sprigs of fresh dill, very finely chopped

generous pinch of sea salt and black pepper

glug of good-quality extra virgin olive oil

1 crusty white bread stick (my favourite is tiger bread), cut into 1cm (½in) thick slices

**1** In a bowl, stir together the tomatoes, chopped basil and dill and season with salt and pepper. Stir in a generous glug of olive oil.

**2** Lay the slices of bread onto the hot grill and toast for 2 minutes until grill marks appear, then use tongs to flip the slices over and toast for 2 minutes on the other side.

**3** Remove from the barbecue and place on a serving plate. Top with the tomato mix and serve while the toast is hot.

**HOT TIP**

Use a mix of ripe baby tomatoes for colour and flavour – think red, green and orange. Many supermarkets sell mixed packs, or choose your own selections.

# OLIVE FLATBREADS

**BARBECUE COOKING TEMPERATURE:** high heat

**MAKES** 4

Homemade flatbreads are easy to make and are delicious cooked on the barbecue; not only do they take on the smoked flavour but they rise gently, perfect for serving with tamarind aubergines (page 30) or herby meatballs in arrabbiata sauce (page 51). Eat fresh, straight from the grill.

300g (2½ cups) strong white bread flour, plus extra for dusting

7g (¼oz) fast-action dried yeast

1 tsp sea salt

pinch of sugar

1 tbsp olive oil, plus extra for brushing

2 tbsp plain soya yogurt

6 pitted green olives, sliced

Pictured overleaf

**1** In a large bowl, stir together the flour, yeast, salt and sugar until combined.

**2** Stir in the olive oil, soya yogurt and 120ml (½ cup) warm water and combine until a dough is formed.

**3** Sprinkle some flour on a clean work surface, turn out the dough and knead for 10 minutes.

**4** Cut the dough into 4 even pieces (cut in half, then halve each piece). Place the bowl over the dough and leave to rise in a warm place for 30 minutes.

**5** Remove the bowl, and gently press a quarter of the olives into each piece, kneading gently until combined. Flatten with your hands or use a rolling pin to gently press the flatbreads.

**6** Brush both sides with a little olive oil, then carefully place onto the hot grill. Cook for 4–5 minutes on each side until lightly browned and risen. Best eaten hot.

**HOT TIP**

Swap the olives for fresh herbs, including dill and parsley, or stir in sundried tomatoes for variations on this classic grilled bread.

# BROWN SUGAR BEANS

**BARBECUE COOKING TEMPERATURE:**
high-medium heat. Move some of the charcoal to the side so part of the grill has indirect heat.

**SERVES** 4 generously

1 tbsp sunflower oil
1 onion, thinly sliced
1 red (bell) pepper, deseeded and diced
2 tsp soft brown sugar
1 tsp dried oregano
1 tsp smoked paprika
pinch of ground cinnamon
500g (2 cups) passata (sieved tomatoes)
2 x 400g (14oz) cans of butter (lima) beans, drained and rinsed
1 tbsp brown sauce
generous pinch of sea salt
handful of fresh flat-leaf parsley, finely chopped

Pictured on pages 56–57

Infuse these rich, sweet baked beans with smoke from the barbecue, for layers of flavour that an oven just can't deliver on. Cover with the barbecue lid to develop a sticky, thick sauce that is comforting and moreish. Serve with peanut butter and chilli jam bean burgers with pretzels (page 55).

**1** Add the oil to a 30cm (12in) carbon steel pan (barbecue-safe) and place onto the grill where the direct heat is. Add the onion and red pepper and slowly caramelize for about 8–10 minutes until softened and the onion turns golden brown.

**2** Add the sugar, oregano, smoked paprika and cinnamon and cook for a further 2 minutes.

**3** Pour in the passata, butter beans and brown sauce and stir until the beans are combined in the sauce.

**4** Move the pan over the indirect heat area and place the lid of the barbecue down, or cover with kitchen foil if your barbecue doesn't have a lid. Cook for 35–40 minutes, stirring a couple of times, until bubbling and thickened.

**5** Remove from the grill and sprinkle over a pinch of salt. Scatter with chopped parsley just before serving.

### HOT TIP

British-style brown sauce gives depth of flavour and a touch of spice; if you don't have any available, add 1 teaspoon tamarind paste with a pinch of mild chilli powder.

# STICKY BROCCOLI
## WITH SOY, CHILLI AND SESAME

**BARBECUE COOKING
TEMPERATURE:**
medium heat

**SERVES** 4

4 tbsp soy sauce
1 tbsp sunflower oil
pinch of dried chilli flakes
200g (7oz) Tenderstem
  broccoli
1 tbsp sesame seeds
sea salt

Tenderstem is my favourite type of broccoli to cook on the
barbecue, as the whole of the vegetable can be eaten, and
the edges become crisp and charred on the grill. Marinate
for at least 2 hours before grilling, for an intense flavour and
addictive stickiness.

**1** In a large bowl, whisk
together the soy sauce,
oil and chilli flakes. Add
the broccoli and toss to
ensure it is coated. Allow to
marinate for at least 2 hours.

**2** Thread the broccoli onto
one or two metal skewers.
Place onto the hot grill
for 5–6 minutes, turning
a couple of times, until the
broccoli is tender and sticky.

**3** Carefully remove the
cooked broccoli from the
skewers onto a serving
plate. Scatter with sea salt.

**HOT TIP**

This dish is delicious served
either hot or cold. Throw in
some cooked edamame,
peanuts and watercress
for a side salad to impress.

# GRILLED ASPARAGUS
## WITH ORANGE AND BLACK PEPPER

**BARBECUE COOKING TEMPERATURE:**
medium heat

**SERVES** 2

Give distinctive fresh asparagus layers of flavour by cooking on the barbecue, before dressing in orange, chives and feisty black pepper. Serve hot or chilled, as a delicious side dish or spooned over a leafy green salad.

zest and juice of 1 unwaxed
   orange
handful of fresh chives,
   finely chopped
generous pinch of black
   pepper
250g (9oz) asparagus spears,
   woody ends discarded
1 tbsp olive oil
generous pinch of sea salt

Also pictured on page 68

**1** In a bowl, stir together the orange zest and juice, chives and black pepper. Set aside.

**2** Slide the asparagus spears onto metal skewers. It works best to skewer the tougher stem rather than the tip. Brush generously with olive oil.

**3** Place the skewers onto the grill, over indirect heat. Cook for 8–10 minutes until tender and just charred, turning a few times.

**4** Remove the skewers from the grill and carefully slide the cooked asparagus spears into the bowl of dressing. Toss in the orange dressing until coated, then spoon onto a serving plate. Scatter with sea salt.

**HOT TIP**

Cooking the asparagus on skewers means easier turning and a more even cook; the spears are also less likely to fall between the grill bars.

# SALT-BAKED POTATOES

**BARBECUE COOKING TEMPERATURE:**
medium-high heat

**SERVES** 4

Jacket potatoes as they should be – crisp and full of flavour on the outside, fluffy and light inside, with a wonderful smoked and salted taste throughout. The first stage of the cooking process allows steam to circulate in the foil until the potatoes are tender, then cooking directly on the hot grill really crisps up the skin. Delicious served with brown sugar beans (page 78), or simply with vegan butter.

4 large baking potatoes, washed clean and dried thoroughly
4 tbsp olive oil
4 tsp flaked sea salt

Pictured on pages 56–57

**1** Lay out 8 pieces of foil, large enough to wrap each potato.

**2** Prick the potatoes all over with a fork, then rub each potato with 1 tablespoon olive oil.

**3** Sprinkle 1 teaspoon salt evenly over each potato, wrap in a piece of foil, then firmly double-wrap with another piece.

**4** Place the wrapped potatoes onto the grill. Cook for 1 hour, turning every 10 minutes, then use tongs to remove and discard the foil. Place the potatoes on the grill for a further 10 minutes, turning a couple of times until crisp all over.

**HOT TIP**

I've been known to batch cook these potatoes then freeze them; simply defrost and reheat when nothing but a smoky, salt-baked jacket potato will do.

# CORIANDER BUTTER CORN ON THE COB
## WITH LIME

**BARBECUE COOKING TEMPERATURE:**
medium-high heat

**SERVES** 4

4 corn on the cob, outer husk removed

4 rounded tsp vegan butter, softened to room temperature

handful of fresh coriander (cilantro), roughly torn

2 rounded tsp sea salt

2 unwaxed limes, halved

Pictured on pages 21 and 40–41

So simple but utterly delicious, you can prepare the corn in advance, then just pop the parcels on the barbecue when you are ready to cook. So versatile, they'll go with pretty much anything.

**1** Lay out 8 squares of kitchen foil for double-wrapping the corn, making sure that each one is large enough to securely fit around the cob. Place each corn on the cob into a double layer of foil.

**2** In a small bowl, stir together the butter, coriander and salt, then spoon a generous rounded teaspoon of the mixture onto each corn on the cob. Place half a lime into the foil packet at the side of each cob, then securely seal both layers of foil.

**3** Cook on the barbecue for 30–35 minutes, turning frequently, until tender.

**HOT TIP**

Serve as whole corn on the cob straight from the hot foil packets, or slice down the length of the cooked corn on the cob to release the sweetcorn kernels to serve in a bowl or scattered over a salad.

# TOASTED ALMOND AND ORANGE PILAU RICE

**FROM THE KITCHEN**

**SERVES** 4

Make this rice dish ahead of time on the kitchen hob, and serve in a sharing bowl for guests to tuck in! It's delicious served as a hot or cold dish with any barbecue combinations, but is particularly good served with spiced yogurt cauliflower and mango (page 44) and spicy potato salad (page 120).

300g (1½ cups) white basmati rice
500ml (2 cups) hot vegetable stock
½ tsp ground turmeric
1 cinnamon stick
2 dried bay leaves
2 tbsp flaked almonds
juice of ½ unwaxed orange
generous pinch of sea salt
small handful of fresh coriander (cilantro), chopped

**1** Add the rice, vegetable stock, turmeric, cinnamon stick and bay leaves to a pan and bring to the boil over a medium heat on the hob. Cook for 15 minutes, stirring occasionally to avoid sticking.

**2** When all of the stock has been absorbed, remove from the heat. Place a lid securely on the pan and allow to stand for 10 minutes.

**3** Meanwhile, toast the flaked almonds in a dry pan for 2–3 minutes until golden and toasted. Set aside.

**4** Uncover the pan and remove the bay leaves and cinnamon stick. Fork through the rice to make it fluffy, then stir in the orange juice and season with sea salt. Stir in the coriander and toasted almonds and serve.

**HOT TIP**

If you're serving this rice dish cold, allow it to cool to room temperature before putting into the fridge. It is best (and safest) to enjoy this rice dish the day it is prepared, or the following day if kept chilled; if you want to serve it warm make sure it is thoroughly reheated.

# BARBECUE PATATAS BRAVAS

**BARBECUE COOKING TEMPERATURE:** high heat

**SERVES** 4

Patatas bravas is a tapas classic, and sits right at home on a sizzling barbecue. This dish is perfect with drinks, as an appetizer, to serve as your guests arrive. Delicious with smoky paella with butter beans and olives (page 36) and grilled fennel, orange and dill salad (page 133).

**For the potatoes**
12 baby potatoes
1 tbsp olive oil

**For the sauce**
1 tbsp olive oil
1 onion, diced
2 garlic cloves, crushed
1 tsp sweet paprika
generous pinch of dried chilli flakes
300g (10oz) passata (sieved tomatoes)
pinch of sugar
small handful of fresh flat-leaf parsley, finely chopped
generous pinch of sea salt and black pepper

Pictured overleaf

**1** Bring a large pan of salted water to the boil on the hob, then add the baby potatoes. Par-boil for 7–8 minutes until just tender. Drain away the water and pat the potatoes dry using kitchen paper or a clean kitchen cloth.

**2** Thread the par-boiled potatoes on metal skewers (approximately 6 per skewer) and brush with olive oil. Set aside.

**3** Add the oil to a 30cm (12in) carbon steel pan (barbecue-safe) and place on the grill. When the oil is hot, add the onion and cook for 2–3 minutes until it begins to soften. Add the garlic, paprika and chilli flakes and cook for a further minute, stirring constantly to avoid burning.

**4** Pour in the passata and sugar, then simmer over a medium heat for around 10 minutes, stirring occasionally. Remove from the heat and stir in the chopped parsley. Season to taste with salt and pepper.

**5** At this stage, the barbecue will have cooled to a medium heat temperature, where the embers are glowing. Carefully place the skewers of potatoes on the grill and cook for 10 minutes, turning frequently, until browned and softened.

**6** Remove from the grill and use tongs to push the potatoes from the skewers onto a serving plate. Drizzle with the sauce and serve hot.

### HOT TIP

The sauce can be prepared up to 3 days in advance, then kept in the fridge in a sealed container. Simply reheat in a pan or the microwave until piping hot.

# SALT AND VINEGAR PADRON PEPPERS

**BARBECUE COOKING TEMPERATURE:**
medium heat

**SERVES** 2

'Some are hot, and some are not' is the traditional mantra when eating Padron peppers, as within a bowl of these generally mild peppers, you'll often come across a really fierce one! The vinegar adds a hint of acidity to the blistered skins – use sparingly to enhance the flavour. Delicious served with drinks, or as tapas alongside barbecue patatas bravas (page 86).

135g (4½oz) fresh Padron peppers
1 tsp olive oil
generous pinch of sea salt
a few drops of malt vinegar

Pictured on page 17 and overleaf

**1** Brush the Padron peppers with olive oil, then place onto the hot grill. Cook for about 8–10 minutes until blistered and blackened in some spots.

**2** Use tongs to place into a serving dish. Scatter with salt and sprinkle over a few drops of malt vinegar. Serve hot.

**HOT TIP**

Serve with the stems attached, holding the stem while you bite into the pepper. One bite is the traditional way!

# ITALIAN BAKED BEANS

**BARBECUE COOKING TEMPERATURE:**
medium heat

**SERVES** 2 generously

Simmer these easy Italian baked beans on the barbecue, then serve hot, with a ladle so everyone can tuck in. They're also suitable for freezing – just leave to cool, transfer to a freezerproof container and freeze for up to 3 months. Delicious as a side to Mediterranean sausages (page 48) with marinated antipasti (page 73) and charred courgettes with lemon and dill yogurt (page 97).

1 tbsp olive oil

1 onion, diced

4 long leaves of cavolo nero, roughly chopped and tough stems discarded

2 garlic cloves

pinch of dried chilli flakes

pinch of dried sage

500g (2 cups) passata (sieved tomatoes)

pinch of sugar

2 x 400g (14oz) cans of cannellini beans, drained and rinsed

generous pinch of sea salt and black pepper

**1** Add the oil to a 30cm (12in) carbon steel (barbecue-safe) pan and place onto the grill. When it is hot, add the onion and cavolo nero and cook for 3–5 minutes until softened. Stir in the garlic, chilli flakes and sage and cook for a further minute until fragrant.

**2** Add the passata, sugar and cannellini beans and simmer for 15–20 minutes, stirring frequently.

**3** Remove from the heat and season to taste with salt and plenty of pepper.

**HOT TIP**

A pinch of sugar reduces the acidity of the passata – granulated or caster (superfine) sugar will work fine.

# RATATOUILLE FOIL PARCELS

**BARBECUE COOKING TEMPERATURE:**
medium-high heat

**SERVES** 4

Ratatouille is the perfect way to celebrate the vegetables of the season, and these individual foil parcels are an easy and mess-free way to enjoy the flavours of this classic French dish. The vegetables steam in the foil parcels, giving perfect results every time. Serve in the foil, for your guests to unwrap and enjoy alongside Mediterranean sausages (page 48) and squash, apple and chestnut mushroom skewers (page 59).

1 courgette (zucchini), sliced into half-rounds

1 red onion, quartered

1 red (bell) pepper, deseeded and roughly sliced

8 pitted green olives

4 orange or yellow cherry tomatoes

1 large tomato, quartered

4 tbsp olive oil

1 tsp dried oregano

generous pinch of sea salt and black pepper

handful of small, fresh basil leaves

**1** In a bowl, toss together the courgette, onion, pepper, olives and tomatoes.

**2** Stir in the olive oil and oregano, then season with salt and plenty of pepper.

**3** Lay out 8 pieces of foil. Spoon the vegetable mix evenly into the middle of 4 of the pieces, making sure the vegetables are distributed evenly, then scatter the veg with the basil leaves. Wrap in another piece of foil and fold into the middle firmly to enlose the veg.

**4** Place the foil parcels onto the grill and cook for 15–20 minutes until the vegetables have softened. Serve hot.

**HOT TIP**

The vegetables can be combined with olive oil and oregano up to a day in advance and kept in the fridge, then spooned into foil just before grilling.

# GARDEN TOMATO TART

**FROM THE KITCHEN**

**SERVES** 4

Simple, fresh and elegant, this tomato tart is cooked in advance and served warm or cold for a taste of the summer – it makes a fail-safe addition to any al fresco event! Cook the tomatoes separately to the pastry base, to avoid any 'soggy bottom'. Choose mixed colour heritage tomatoes, from green to yellow to red. The tomatoes can be placed on a barbecue-safe carbon steel baking tray and cooked on the hot grill for a smokier flavour, but I love the freshness of this dish as an accompaniment to other grilled food. It's also a great dish to take to a barbecue potluck!

1 x 320g (11oz) sheet of ready-rolled puff pastry (ensure dairy-free)

1 garlic clove, bruised

4 large mixed tomatoes, sliced

6 small mixed tomatoes, sliced

drizzle of olive oil

small handful of fresh dill, finely chopped

a few nasturtium leaves and flowers (optional)

generous pinch of sea salt and black pepper

Also pictured on page 11

**1** Preheat the oven to 200°C/400°F/gas mark 6.

**2** Unroll the pastry onto a baking tray (keeping it on the greaseproof paper it is wrapped in under the pastry, or line a baking tray with baking parchment), then fold in the edges by 2cm (¾in) all round to create a border. Rub the garlic clove over the centre of the pastry then discard. Prick the centre of the pastry with a fork a few times.

**3** Place the tomatoes on another baking tray and drizzle with olive oil.

**4** Place both baking trays in the oven for 12–15 minutes until the pastry is risen and golden.

**5** Remove both trays from the oven. If the centre of the pastry has risen up in places, push it down gently with a fork. Lay the tomatoes onto the pastry. Scatter with dill, some nasturtium leaves and flowers, if you like, and a pinch of sea salt. Serve warm or cold.

**HOT TIP**

Many brands of shop-bought puff pastry are vegan friendly, as the pastry contains vegetable fat instead of dairy butter. Always check the ingredients before you buy.

# GARLIC NAAN BREADS

**BARBECUE COOKING
TEMPERATURE:** high heat

**MAKES** 6

Good things come to those who wait, and these homemade garlic naan breads are definitely worth waiting for. Buttery, charred and so fluffy, these naan breads are perfect for sharing, dipping and indulging in! Serve with spiced yogurt cauliflower and mango (page 44), spicy potato salad (page 120) and carrot, coriander and toasted cashew salad (page 114).

7g (¼oz) dried yeast

2 tsp granulated sugar

300g (2½ cups) strong white bread flour, plus extra for dusting

2 tsp nigella seeds

1 tbsp sunflower oil, plus extra for brushing

4 rounded tbsp plain soya yogurt

1 rounded tbsp vegan butter

2 garlic cloves, crushed

small handful of fresh flat-leaf parsley, finely chopped

generous pinch of sea salt

**1** Add the yeast to a jug with 100ml (scant ½ cup) warm water and 1 teaspoon of the sugar. Stir gently then set aside for 15 minutes until frothy.

**2** In a bowl, stir together the flour, nigella seeds and remaining sugar. Add the oil and yogurt, along with the frothy yeast mix. Bring together into a soft dough. Add a sprinkle of water if the dough seems dry, or a sprinkle of flour if the mixture is too sticky.

**3** Lightly flour a clean work surface, then knead the dough for 10 minutes.

**4** Brush a large, clean bowl with a little oil and place the kneaded dough in it. Cover with cling film (plastic wrap) or a tea towel, and leave to prove in a warm place for about 1 hour, or until doubled in size.

**5** Remove the dough from the bowl and cut into 6 even pieces. Roll out the balls into oval shapes, around 20cm (8in) in length, slightly wider at the bottom than the top.

**6** Place each naan bread on a piece of foil but don't cover the top. Working in batches, place the foil and naan breads onto the hot grill. Cook for 5 minutes until the breads rise a little, then carefully flip them over to cook the other sides. Repeat until all of the naan breads are cooked.

**7** Melt the butter in a pan on the hob or in a microwave. Stir in the garlic, chopped parsley and salt. Liberally brush the garlic butter over both sides of the naan breads. Serve warm.

### HOT TIP

Prepare and cook these naan breads in advance if you prefer: cook them in a dry pan on the hob for 4–5 minutes on each side, then simply finish off by placing them directly onto the barbecue grill for a minute before brushing with garlic butter.

# PECAN AND APPLE SALAD
## WITH CHARRED CARROTS

**BARBECUE COOKING TEMPERATURE:** high heat

**SERVES** 4

Never overlook the humble carrot: this versatile vegetable becomes sweet and smoky after grilling, with a depth of flavour that no other cooking method can bring out. Team hot, charred carrots with crisp apples, pecans and dill for a salad that everyone will love.

60g (2oz) fresh wild rocket (arugula)

2 green apples, thinly sliced

1 celery stalk, finely chopped

3 tbsp pecans, roughly chopped

1 tbsp dried cranberries

handful of fresh flat-leaf parsley, roughly torn

2 tbsp good-quality olive oil, plus 1 tbsp extra for brushing

squeeze of juice from 1 unwaxed lemon

4 large carrots, peeled, green tops trimmed, halved lengthwise

generous pinch of sea salt and black pepper

Pictured on pages 40–41

**1** In a large bowl, toss together the rocket, apples, celery, pecans, cranberries and parsley. Drizzle in the 2 tablespoons olive oil and stir in the lemon juice.

**2** Brush the carrots with the 1 tablespoon olive oil, then place on the hot grill. Cook for about 5–6 minutes on each side until char lines appear and the carrots have softened.

**3** Remove from the grill and place over the salad. Season with salt and plenty of pepper and serve while the carrots are hot.

**HOT TIP**

Change things up with various coloured carrots (including purple!) or with baby carrots large enough to sit across the grill. Adjust the cooking times for smaller carrots, and allow char lines to appear before turning.

# CHARRED COURGETTES
## WITH LEMON AND DILL YOGURT

**BARBECUE COOKING
TEMPERATURE:**
medium heat

**SERVES** 4

2 rounded tbsp plain soya
    yogurt
juice of ¼ unwaxed lemon
small handful of fresh dill,
    finely chopped
generous pinch of sea salt
2 courgettes (zucchini),
    thinly sliced
1 tbsp olive oil
pinch of black pepper

Lightly charring courgettes give a whole new depth to the vegetable, making them a sublime seasonal side dish for any al fresco supper. Top with spoonfuls of fragrant savoury yogurt. Delicious as a side to no-lobster rolls (page 52).

**1** In a bowl, whisk together the yogurt and lemon juice, then stir in the dill. Season with salt and set aside.

**2** Brush both sides of the courgette slices with olive oil, then carefully place on the hot grill. Cook on each side for 5–6 minutes until char lines appear and the slices have softened.

**3** Use tongs to remove the courgette from the grill and place onto a serving plate. Season with black pepper and spoon over the lemon and dill yogurt.

**HOT TIP**

Throw the charred courgettes over wild rocket, torn basil leaves and toasted pine nuts for a warm salad that makes the perfect summer lunch.

# CANDY-STRIPE ONIONS

**BARBECUE COOKING TEMPERATURE:**
medium heat

**SERVES** 4

1 large brown onion, left whole but ends removed
1 large red onion, left whole but ends removed
1 tbsp olive oil
1 tsp maple syrup
pinch of sea salt

Also pictured on pages 18 and 56–57

Serve these barbecued red and white onions on the cooking skewers, so guests can help themselves to sweet, soft onions to top burgers and sausages, as well as as an accompaniment to Caribbean cauliflower with pineapple and black bean salsa (page 61).

**1** Hold the peeled brown onion down securely on a chopping board. Use a sharp knife to cut the onion horizontally into 2cm (¾in) thick slices, and keep the rings together. Lay the slices flat, and thread a skewer vertically through them; aiming for 3 red onion slices and 3 white onion slices over 2 skewers.

**2** Brush with olive oil, then place on the hot grill for 20 minutes, turning a couple of times.

**3** Brush with a little maple syrup and cook for a further 2–3 minutes on each side until caramelized.

**4** Remove from the grill and season with a pinch of sea salt before sliding off the skewers.

**HOT TIP**

Large onions make larger 'pinwheels' of cooked onions, perfect to place into a burger bun. If you have smaller onions then use two of each, and add more into each burger bun.

# SAGE AND ONION SAUSAGE ROLLS
## WITH KETCHUP

**FROM THE KITCHEN**

**MAKES** 8

Everyone loves a sausage roll, especially when it's eaten al fresco. Bake in advance, then pile them high on a plate for guests to help themselves. I use pre-cooked, vacuum-packed chestnuts (available in supermarkets) to create the vegan sausage filling, flavoured with classic sage and onion.

1 tbsp sunflower oil, plus 2 tsp for brushing

1 small onion, finely diced

1 tsp dried sage

180g (6oz) vacuum-packed cooked chestnuts, finely chopped

generous pinch of sea salt and black pepper

1 x 400g (14oz) can cannellini or butter beans, drained but liquid reserved

1 sheet of shop-bought puff pastry (ensure dairy-free)

2 tsp tomato ketchup, plus extra for serving

Pictured on pages 100–101

**1** Preheat the oven to 200°C/400°F/ gas mark 6 and line 2 baking trays with baking parchment.

**2** Heat 1 tablespoon sunflower oil in a large pan, then add the onion and dried sage. Cook for 2–3 minutes on the hob, stirring frequently, until the onion starts to soften.

**3** Add the chopped chestnuts then cook for another 2 minutes. Season with salt and pepper, then remove from the heat.

**4** Roughly mash the cannellini or butter beans in a bowl using a fork or potato masher, then stir this through the onion and chestnuts. Add a splash of the bean liquid so that the mixture just holds together.

**5** Lay out the sheet of puff pastry on a clean, flat surface. Use a pastry brush to sweep over a little sunflower oil.

**6** Spoon the tomato ketchup in a straight line 4cm (1½in) from the top of the pastry. Spoon the filling mixture on top of the ketchup. Roll the pastry to form a log shape, then crimp the edge with a fork to seal.

**7** Use a sharp knife to cut the roll into about 8 even pieces, then place flat on a baking tray. Brush the tops with a little sunflower oil.

**8** Bake in the oven for 25 minutes until golden and crisp. Serve warm or cold, with extra ketchup for dipping.

### HOT TIP

Many brands of shop-bought pastry are vegan, as they use vegetable fats instead of dairy butter. Always check the ingredients before you buy.

# JERK SWEET POTATO WEDGES

**BARBECUE COOKING TEMPERATURE:**
medium-high heat

**SERVES** 4

2 large sweet potatoes, peeled and chopped into even wedges
1 tbsp sunflower oil
1 tsp jerk seasoning
generous pinch of smoked sea salt

Pictured on pages 18 and 56–57

Everyone loves a handful of spiced sweet potato wedges. These easy-to-cook wedges are crisp and golden with a hint of Jamaican jerk seasoning. I find it easier to cook the wedges on skewers as it makes turning easier, in one simple step, without having to use tongs to individually turn each potato wedge on the grill.

**1** Bring a large pan of water to the boil over a medium-high heat on the hob. Add the sweet potato wedges and par-boil for 5–7 minutes until just tender. Thoroughly drain away the water.

**2** Allow the wedges to cool until you are able to handle them, then pat dry with kitchen paper or a clean cloth to remove as much water as possible. Drizzle with the sunflower oil and rub over the jerk seasoning until evenly coated.

**3** Thread the wedges onto 4 metal skewers, so the flattest surfaces will be able to sit on the grill. Place the skewers onto the hot grill and cook for 10–12 minutes, turning a few times, until the edges are crisp and browned and the middles are cooked through.

**4** Carefully slide the cooked wedges off the skewers and season with a pinch of smoked sea salt.

**HOT TIP**

Par-boiling the wedges for a few minutes softens the potatoes enough to thread onto a skewer, and ensures a more even cook on the barbecue, but don't cook for longer than 5–7 minutes as the wedges will be more likely to break off the skewers when they are placed over the high heat.

# SALADS & EXTRAS

# CHARRED PEPPER ORZO SALAD
## WITH OLIVES

**BARBECUE COOKING TEMPERATURE:**
medium heat

**SERVES** 4

Tender and juicy peppers, orzo pasta, olives, lemon juice and fresh baby cucumbers are combined in this satisfying salad. Ramiro peppers are long and slim and have a thin skin so they cook quickly and become very tender with little effort from you. Be patient and allow the coals to cool a little so the peppers can gently char without blackening too much. Serve either warm or chilled.

2 Ramiro peppers, halved lengthways and deseeded

1 tbsp good-quality olive oil, plus extra for drizzling

250g (9oz) dried orzo pasta (ensure egg-free)

2 baby (mini) cucumbers, thinly sliced (or ¼ regular cucumber, diced)

8 black pitted olives, thinly sliced

1 tbsp flaked (slivered) almonds

juice of ½ unwaxed lemon

handful of fresh flat-leaf parsley, finely chopped

small handful of fresh dill, finely chopped

generous pinch of sea salt and black pepper

**1** Brush the Ramiro peppers all over with olive oil. Place the peppers onto the hot grill and cook for about 5–6 minutes on each side until charred in places and very tender. Remove from the grill and allow to cool while you prepare the salad.

**2** Bring a pan of water to the boil on the hob, then add the orzo. Cook for 8–10 minutes until al dente, then thoroughly drain away the water.

**3** Add the pasta to a large bowl, then stir in the cucumber, olives, almonds, lemon juice, parsley and dill.

**4** Roughly slice the Ramiro peppers, then stir into the salad.

**5** Drizzle with a little extra olive oil and stir gently to combine. Season to taste with salt and pepper.

**HOT TIP**

Many brands of dried orzo pasta are vegan as it uses simple durum wheat semolina with no eggs, but always check the ingredients before you buy.

# KIWI AND AVOCADO SALSA

**FROM THE KITCHEN**

**SERVES** 4

Tangy, zesty and creamy – this salsa really delivers. If you are able to source golden kiwis, their skins are thin and pear-like, so won't need peeling and give extra texture, but standard peeled kiwis are bright and vibrant in this salsa. Unexpected and delicious with sizzling fajitas with charred lime (page 54) or loaded into peanut butter and chilli jam bean burgers with pretzels (page 55).

3 kiwis, peeled and diced
1 avocado, peeled and diced
2 radishes, finely diced
generous handful of fresh coriander (cilantro), finely chopped
handful of fresh flat-leaf parsley, finely chopped
juice of 1 unwaxed lime
pinch of smoked sea salt

**1** In a bowl, stir together the diced kiwis, avocado and radishes.

**2** Stir in the coriander and parsley, then squeeze through the lime juice.

**3** Season to taste with smoked sea salt before stirring to combine.

**HOT TIP**

Add 1 diced green chilli if you like your salsa with some heat!

# WARM GRAPES
## WITH WHIPPED CREAM CHEESE AND CHIVES

**BARBECUE COOKING TEMPERATURE:**
medium heat

**SERVES** 4

Grapes are transformed when grilled, becoming extra juicy and sherbet-flavoured. I love to dip them into a creamy whipped cream cheese, but they are also delicious served as a simple dessert or as an appetizer with a chilled glass of vegan white wine. Serve with a few savoury crackers alongside, if you like.

150g (5oz) pot of vegan cream cheese, chilled

1 tbsp sparking water, chilled

pinch of sea salt and black pepper

handful of fresh chives, finely chopped

500g (1lb 2oz) red seedless grapes on the vine

1 tbsp olive oil

Pictured on pages 110–111

**1** Scoop the cheese into a bowl and whisk for 2–3 minutes until light in texture. Pour in the sparking water, stir, then whisk for a 2–3 minutes more until fluffy.

**2** Stir in the salt and pepper and chopped chives. Spoon into a serving bowl and chill until served.

**3** Break the bunch of grapes into 4 smaller bunches. Drizzle the grapes with a little olive oil, then place the bunches on the grill for 3–4 minutes, turning often.

**4** Place the bunches of grapes on a serving plate, along with the whipped cheese.

**HOT TIP**

The lightest, 'fluffiest' cream cheese is whipped up with a hand-held electric whisk, but feel free to get busy with a manual balloon whisk for 5–6 minutes.

# GRILLED FENNEL, ORANGE AND DILL SALAD

**BARBECUE COOKING TEMPERATURE:** high heat

**SERVES** 4

If you don't regularly cook with fennel, this is a great way to introduce yourself to the delicate aniseed flavour. Grilling it on a hot barbecue enhances the flavour while retaining some of the texture, which works perfectly with fresh orange segments, olives and creamy butter beans.

2 fennel bulbs, sliced into wedges

1 tbsp olive oil

generous handful of watercress

1 unwaxed orange, peeled and segmented

6 pitted black olives, roughly sliced

small handful of fresh dill, finely chopped

small handful of fresh flat-leaf parsley, finely chopped

400g (14oz) good-quality jarred or canned butter (lima) beans, drained and rinsed

pinch of sea salt and black pepper

Pictured on pages 110–111

**1** Brush the wedges of fennel with a little olive oil, then place onto the hot grill. Cook for 4–5 minutes until char lines appear, then turn and cook for a further 4–5 minutes.

**2** Meanwhile, toss together the watercress, orange segments, olives, dill, parsley and butter beans in a bowl and stir in any remaining olive oil.

**3** Remove the charred fennel from the barbecue and toss into the bowl. Serve hot, warm or cold.

**HOT TIP**

I like to slice the fennel into uneven wedges, so some pieces are more charred than others, with some rawness in the centre for crunch and texture.

# CARROT, CORIANDER AND TOASTED CASHEW SALAD

**FROM THE KITCHEN**

**SERVES** 4

Colourful, vibrant, zingy and crunchy – this salad has it all! Simple to prepare, serve and eat, it's delicious with spiced yogurt cauliflower and mango (page 44) or with mushroom masala sausages (page 64) and garlic naan breads (page 94).

4 carrots, peeled and grated

¼ red cabbage, finely shredded

generous handful of fresh coriander (cilantro) leaves, roughly torn

juice of ½ unwaxed lemon

pinch of sea salt

4 tbsp cashews

**1** In a large bowl, toss together the grated carrots, cabbage and coriander. Squeeze over the lemon juice and add a pinch of salt.

**2** In a dry pan, toast the cashews over a high heat for 1–2 minutes until just browned and fragrant. Toss them into the salad.

**HOT TIP**

It's worth spending a couple of minutes toasting the cashews as this gives layers of flavour to a simple salad. Always use a dry pan over a high heat, and toss them in the pan for a couple of minutes until lightly browned and fragrant.

# CRUNCHY SESAME AND LIME SALAD
## WITH SOY AND EDAMAME

**FROM THE KITCHEN**

**SERVES** 4

This quick-to-prepare salad is a refreshing and zingy addition to any barbecue plate, especially with sweet and sour tofu and pineapple (page 34) and satay Tenderstem, courgette, baby corns and sugarsnaps (page 35). It's as simple as it is delicious!

4 tbsp frozen or fresh edamame beans

½ white cabbage, finely shredded

1 large carrot, peeled and sliced into matchsticks

1 red (bell) pepper, deseeded and thinly sliced

1 celery stalk, finely chopped

generous handful of fresh coriander (cilantro), roughly torn

2 tbsp soy sauce

juice of ½ unwaxed lime

1 tbsp sesame seeds

1 tbsp roasted peanuts

Pictured on pages 122–123

**1** Bring a small pan of water to the boil over a high heat and throw in the edamame beans. Cook for 3–4 minutes until tender, then drain away the water and set the beans aside.

**2** In a large bowl, toss together the cabbage, carrot, pepper, celery and coriander.

**3** Stir in the soy sauce and lime juice, then scatter in the cooked edamame beans. Stir in the sesame seeds and peanuts, distributing evenly.

**HOT TIP**

This salad will last for up to 3 days when refrigerated in a sealed container.

# NUTTY RICE SALAD

**FROM THE KITCHEN**

**SERVES** 4

Keep things simple with a fresh and crunchy rice salad, which is versatile enough to serve with a variety of main dishes. It's especially delicious with teriyaki tofu with charred greens (page 33) and grill-side katsu burger with wasabi mayo (page 62). Serve hot or chilled.

300g (1½ cups) white basmati rice
pinch of sea salt
2 spring onions (scallions), finely chopped
handful of fresh coriander (cilantro) leaves, chopped
100g (¾ cup) salted and roasted peanuts, roughly chopped
juice of 2 unwaxed limes

**1** Add the rice and 500ml (2 cups) water to a large pan and cook over a medium-high heat on the hob for 10 minutes until the water has absorbed.

**2** Remove from the heat and place a tight-fitting lid on the pan. Allow it to stand for 10 minutes.

**3** Remove the lid, fork through the rice to fluff it up and stir in a pinch of sea salt. Stir in the spring onions, coriander and chopped peanuts until evenly distributed.

**4** Stir in the lime juice and serve either hot or chilled.

**HOT TIP**

Basmati rice has a quick cooking time, so it's the perfect rice for a salad. I allow the rice to stand for a few minutes after cooking, to absorb any extra liquid, making it fluffy and light before adding in the extra ingredients.

# PISTACHIO, POMEGRANATE AND MINT SALAD
## WITH BULGAR AND ORANGE

**FROM THE KITCHEN**

**SERVES** 4

Serve this vibrant salad on a sharing plate, so everyone can tuck in! It's colourful, fruity and full of flavours that work perfectly against the slight sourness of tamarind aubergines (page 30). This salad will keep for up to 3 days in the fridge.

100g (½ cup) bulgar wheat

30g (1oz) fresh flat-leaf parsley, finely chopped

generous handful of fresh mint leaves, finely chopped

seeds of 1 pomegranate

5cm (2in) piece of cucumber, diced

4 tbsp shelled pistachios, roughly chopped

juice of ½ unwaxed orange

drizzle of good-quality extra virgin olive oil

pinch of sea salt

Also pictured on page 76–77

**1** Add the bulgar wheat to a bowl and pour over enough boiling water to just cover it. Place a plate over the bowl and leave to stand for 10–15 minutes until the water has been absorbed.

**2** Use a fork to fluff through the bulgar wheat, then stir through the parsley, mint, pomegranate seeds, cucumber and pistachios.

**3** Stir through the orange juice and olive oil until evenly distributed. Season to taste with sea salt.

**HOT TIP**

To make this salad speedier, buy pomegranate seeds and pre-shelled pistachios from the supermarket. Less time and less mess!

# SPICY POTATO SALAD

**FROM THE KITCHEN**

**SERVES** 6

Give a classic potato salad a spicy twist, with mustard seeds, coriander and red onion, coated in a cooling coconut yogurt. Perfect as part of any summer barbecue, but particularly good with mushroom masala sausages (page 64) garlic naan breads (page 94) and carrot, coriander and toasted cashew salad (page 114). Serve warm or chilled.

750g (1lb 10oz) new potatoes, halved
1 tbsp sunflower oil
1 red onion, thinly sliced
1 tsp ground turmeric
½ tsp ground cumin
½ tsp mustard seeds
pinch of chilli flakes
juice of ½ unwaxed lemon
3 rounded tbsp dairy-free coconut yogurt
handful of fresh coriander (cilantro), torn
small handful of fresh chives, finely chopped
pinch of sea salt

**1** Bring a large pan of water to the boil over a medium-high heat on the hob. Add the potatoes and cook for 15–18 minutes until tender.

**2** Add the oil and onion to another pan and soften for 4–5 minutes over a medium heat. Stir in the turmeric, cumin, mustard seeds and chilli flakes and cook for a further 2 minutes.

**3** Thoroughly drain the water from the potatoes and tip them into a bowl. Stir in the spiced onion and oil from the other pan.

**4** Squeeze in the lemon juice and stir in the coconut yoghurt, coriander, chives and sea salt. Allow to infuse for a few minutes before serving.

**HOT TIP**

For a regular potato salad, simply stir 3 tablespoons of vegan mayonnaise into 750g (1lb 10oz) cooked new potatoes along with 2 chopped spring onions (scallions) and a handful of chopped fresh mint. Finish with a squeeze of lemon juice from an unwaxed lemon.

# GRILLED AND PICKLED BABY CUCUMBERS

**BARBECUE COOKING TEMPERATURE:**
medium heat

**SERVES** 4

When barbecued, cucumbers are transformed from mild and cool accompaniments to sweet, flavourful stars-of-the-show! I love to pickle them, as a crunchy, charred alternative to gherkins with burgers, or throw them into a simple leafy salad for an unexpected burst of flavour.

8 baby (mini) cucumbers, halved lengthways
1 tsp sunflower oil
6 tbsp cider vinegar
generous pinch of sea salt
small handful of fresh dill, roughly torn

Pictured on page 104 and overleaf

**1**  Thread the baby cucumber halves onto metal skewers and brush with oil. Place the skewers onto the grill, cut-side down, and grill for about 5–6 minutes until char lines appear. Turn the skewers and cook the cucumbers on the skin side.

**2**  Remove the skewers from the grill, and carefully slide the cucumbers into a bowl. Stir in the cider vinegar, sea salt and dill. Allow to stand for at least 1 hour before enjoying.

**HOT TIP**

Feel free to add the hot, grilled baby cucumbers directly to a salad or as a side to any other grilled food, as an alternative to pickling. Simply remove from the grill and sprinkle with sea salt before enjoying hot.

# DUKKAH

This Middle Eastern nut and spice mix has a toasted flavour, and plenty of crunch. It's a versatile addition to your barbecue feast, as well as being quick and easy to prepare. Perfect to liven up shop-bought houmous, add crunch to grilled pittas, or sprinkled over tamarind aubergines (page 30) to take them to the next level.

4 tbsp blanched hazelnuts
4 tbsp flaked almonds
2 tbsp sunflower seeds
2 tsp cumin seeds
2 tsp fennel seeds
2 tsp coriander seeds
pinch of sea salt

Pictured on pages 76–77

**1** Add the hazelnuts, almonds, sunflower seeds, cumin seeds, fennel seeds and coriander seeds to a dry pan. Toast on the hob for 3–5 minutes, tossing them occasionally to prevent burning, until fragrant and lightly browned.

**2** Pulse in a high-powered blender or food processor until roughly chopped. Season with a pinch of sea salt and then serve in a bowl so guests can help themselves.

**HOT TIP**

Store in a clean, dry jar in a cool place for up to a month – if you can resist it for that long!

# QUICK PINK PICKLES

**FROM THE KITCHEN**

**SERVES** 4 generously

These crunchy, tangy and very pink pickles will brighten any barbecue dish and lift any simple salad. Load into wraps or taco shells, or spoon into grill-side katsu burgers with wasabi mayo (page 62). These pickles will last for up to 5 days when kept in the fridge in a sealed jar (when fully cooled).

1 large red onion, thinly sliced
4 radishes, thinly sliced into
   half-rounds
1 tsp sea salt
¼ tsp dried chilli flakes
6 tbsp cider vinegar

Pictured on pages 76–77
   and 122–123

**1** Put the sliced onion and radishes into a heatproof bowl and pour over enough warm water to cover them.

**2** Cook in the microwave for 5 minutes, then carefully drain away all of the water. (If you don't have a microwave, simply simmer in a pan of boiling water for about 15 minutes, then drain thoroughly.)

**3** Stir in the salt and chilli flakes, then stir through the cider vinegar. Allow to stand for at least 1 hour. Keep in the fridge until ready to use.

**HOT TIP**

After softening the onions and radishes in the microwave, they will temporarily lose some of their pink colour, however this will return and intensify when they have been soaked in vinegar and allowed to stand for at least 1 hour.

# BEETROOT, YOGURT AND ORANGE DIP

**FROM THE KITCHEN**

**SERVES** 4

This gently spiced dip has it all: cool yogurt, earthy beetroot, zesty orange and crunchy pine nuts. But best of all – it's pink! Serve as a light side dish with crudités, as a vibrant alternative to houmous.

2 tsp olive oil

1 garlic clove, crushed

2 tsp pine nuts

½ tsp ground cumin

pinch of dried chilli flakes

300g (10oz) vacuum-packed cooked beetroots (beets)

4 rounded tbsp soya Greek-style yogurt, chilled

zest of 1 unwaxed orange, finely grated

squeeze of juice from 1 unwaxed orange

pinch of sea salt

**1** Add the oil, garlic, pine nuts, ground cumin and chilli flakes to a pan and cook over a low-medium heat for 2–3 minutes until the garlic is soft and the oil is fragranced. Set aside.

**2** Add the beetroots and yogurt into a high-powered jug blender or food processor and blitz until smooth and combined. Stir in the orange zest and juice, then blitz again to combine.

**3** Stir in the garlic and pine nut mix and season to taste with sea salt. Serve in a dipping bowl.

**HOT TIP**

Vegan Greek-style yogurt is available in most supermarkets but if you don't have any available, soya-based yogurt makes a good substitute (compared with oat or coconut yogurt). The dip won't be as thick but will still have a smooth and creamy texture.

# DELI PICKLE MAYO

**FROM THE KITCHEN**

**SERVES** 4 generously

Tangy, crunchy and oh-so-creamy, this mayo is loaded with deli counter favourites including gherkins, pickled onions and capers. Reassuringly familiar when served with vegan burgers and sausages, and the perfect addition to your barbecue feast.

4 rounded tbsp vegan
   mayonnaise
4 pickled gherkins, roughly
   diced, plus 1 tbsp of the
   jarred gherkin pickling
   vinegar
4 mini pickled onions,
   quartered
2 tbsp capers, drained of brine
handful of fresh dill, finely
   chopped
pinch of sea salt

Pictured on pages 25 and
   56–57

**1** In a bowl, stir together the mayonnaise, gherkins and 1 tablespoon of the pickling vinegar from the jar of gherkins. Stir in the pickled onions and capers.

**2** Lightly stir in the fresh dill, then season to taste with salt. Spoon into a serving bowl.

**HOT TIP**

Vegan mayonnaise is readily available these days and most supermarkets will have more than one option, from leading brands to cost-effective own brands.

# GRILLED GUACAMOLE

**BARBECUE COOKING TEMPERATURE:**
medium heat

**SERVES** 4

4 just-ripe avocados, halved and stone removed (leave unpeeled)
4 cherry tomatoes, roughly diced
2 spring onions (scallions), finely chopped
juice of ½ unwaxed lime
small handful of fresh coriander (cilantro), finely chopped
generous pinch of sea salt
1 tsp olive oil

Pictured on pages 40–41

Serve homemade guacamole in hot, grilled avocado halves for a fun new way to enjoy avocados. Allow the hot barbecue to infuse the avocados with a smoky flavour before spooning in plenty of zingy guac. Serve with tortilla chips, sizzling fajitas with charred lime (page 54) or any vegan burger you fancy.

**1** Scoop the flesh from 2 of the avocados and mash until semi-smooth in a bowl. Stir in the tomatoes, spring onions, lime juice and coriander. Season to taste with salt.

**2** Brush the flesh of the remaining 2 avocados with olive oil. Leave the skin intact. Place the avocados flesh-side down on the hot grill for 3–5 minutes and cook until char lines appear.

**3** Remove from the grill and load the stone cavity generously with guacamole.

**HOT TIP**

Be generous when loading the guacamole, but if there's any extra left over, freeze in ice-cube trays and melt over tacos or chilli another time.

# ·SWEET· ·TREATS·

# BARBECUE BANOFFEE PIE

**BARBECUE COOKING TEMPERATURE:**
medium heat

**SERVES** 4 generously

When you think vegan banoffee pie can't get any better, use this method to cook the bananas and toffee sauce on the barbecue, so they soak up the smoky flavours and gently caramelize. This dessert is simple but very impressive. Make sure your can of coconut milk is full-fat (low-fat varieties will become watery instead of whipped) and serve immediately after whipping the coconut cream to prevent it from melting.

1 x 400ml (14fl oz) can of full-fat coconut milk

150g (5oz) vegan butter

200g (7oz) vegan digestive biscuits (graham crackers)

3 bananas, peeled and sliced lengthways

1 tbsp flaked (slivered) almonds

6 tbsp maple syrup

2 rounded tbsp soft light brown sugar

pinch of grated nutmeg

1 square of dark chocolate (ensure dairy-free), grated

## HOT TIP

Many supermarket 'own brands' of digestive biscuits do not contain cow's milk or other animal products, making them suitable for vegans. Always check the ingredients before you buy. Ginger snap biscuits make a delicious alternative to digestive biscuits in this recipe.

**1** Place your can of coconut milk into the fridge overnight. This will separate the coconut cream from the milk, ready for whipping later on in the process.

**2** Line an 18cm (7in) square baking tin with baking parchment (this doesn't need to be a barbecue-safe tin).

**3** Melt the vegan butter over a low heat in a pan on the hob.

**4** Place the digestive biscuits into a clean food-safe bag and break them into a rough crumb with your hands or a rolling pin.

**5** Remove the pan of melted butter from the hob and stir in the biscuit crumbs until combined. Press the mixture into the base of the lined tin and refrigerate for an hour.

**6** Arrange two pieces of foil large enough to securely wrap the bananas. Place the halved bananas into the centre of one piece of foil, then top with the almonds, maple syrup, brown sugar and nutmeg. Scrunch the

foil in to make a parcel and securely wrap with the other piece of foil.

**7** Place the foil parcel onto the hot grill and cook for 15–20 minutes. Remove the parcel from the grill and carefully open from the top – the bananas should be very soft and the syrup bubbling.

**8** Remove the cooled pie base from the fridge and spoon over the bananas and syrup. Return the tin to the fridge for at least 1 hour until fully cooled.

**9** Remove the chilled can of coconut milk from the fridge and open. Spoon out the solidified coconut cream into a bowl (save the clear coconut milk to add to a curry or serve over fruit). Use an electric whisk or stand mixer to whip the cream for 5 minutes until light and smooth.

**10** Remove the tin from the fridge and spoon over the coconut cream just before serving. Scatter with grated chocolate.

# CHOCOLATE FONDUE

**BARBECUE COOKING
TEMPERATURE:** high heat

**SERVES** 6

Bring some family fun to your barbecue with this indulgent chocolate fondue, served with fruit, popcorn, vegan marshmallows and flapjack. Use good-quality vegan milk or dark chocolate for the best flavour and consistency, and ensure the squares are broken into even pieces so they all melt at the same time.

350g (12oz) good-quality milk or dark chocolate (ensure dairy-free)
1 tbsp vegan butter
200ml (generous ¾ cup) vegan single (light) cream

**To serve**
12 strawberries
12 green grapes
12 pieces of sweet popcorn (ensure vegan)
6 vegan marshmallows
6 small squares of vegan flapjack

**1** Break the chocolate into even pieces and place in a 30cm (12in) carbon steel (barbecue-safe) pan. Spoon in the butter and pour in the cream.

**2** Place the pan onto the hot grill and allow the chocolate and butter to melt evenly. Stir occasionally to combine until glossy and melted, which should take 5–10 minutes.

**3** Lay out the strawberries, grapes, popcorn, marshmallows and flapjack onto a sharing board with fondue forks, then enjoy while the chocolate fondue is hot.

**HOT TIP**

For a grown-up chocolate fondue, stir in 2 tablespoons dark rum or amaretto to the hot, melted chocolate, if you like.

# GRILLED LEMON CAKE
## WITH LIMONCELLO CREAM AND PISTACHIOS

**BARBECUE COOKING TEMPERATURE:** high heat

**SERVES** 6

Bake this light and zesty lemon cake in the oven, allow to cool and rest (preferably overnight), then grill on the barbecue to create layers of flavour in a dessert that was made for summer. Whip up a bowl of limoncello-infused vegan cream, then top with crunchy pistachios.

250g (2 cups) self-raising flour

100g (½ cup) caster (superfine) sugar

¾ tsp baking powder

250ml (1 cup) sweetened soya milk

100ml (scant ½ cup) sunflower oil

1 tsp good-quality vanilla extract

zest and juice of ½ unwaxed lemon

270ml (generous 1 cup) vegan double (heavy) cream, chilled

2 tbsp limoncello

2 tbsp shelled pistachios, roughly chopped

Pictured overleaf

**1** Preheat the oven to 180°C/350°F/gas mark 4. Line a small baking tray (30x20cm/12x8in) with baking parchment.

**2** In a large bowl, stir together the flour, sugar and baking powder. In a jug, whisk together the soya milk, sunflower oil, vanilla extract, lemon zest and juice. Fold the liquid mixture into the dry mixture until just combined.

**3** Pour into the lined baking tray, then bake in the oven for 20–25 minutes until lightly golden and risen. Remove from the oven and allow to cool before cutting into 6 squares. Rest the cake overnight, or for at least 6 hours.

**4** When you are ready to serve, add the vegan double cream to a large bowl and stir in the limoncello. Use an electric whisk or stand mixer to beat the cream until whipped and light. Set aside.

**5** Carefully place the squares of cake onto the hot grill. Allow to cook for about 1 minute until char lines appear, then turn them over. Remove from the heat before a golden crust forms on the cake.

**6** Place the grilled cake squares on serving plates and top with a spoonful of the whipped cream. Scatter with chopped pistachios and serve while the cake is still hot.

**HOT TIP**

Vegan double cream is available in most supermarkets, perfect for whipping and versatile enough to use in many desserts and dishes. If you don't have any vegan double cream available, refrigerate a can of full-fat coconut milk overnight and whip the solid separated cream and use this instead.

# CHOCOLATE MOUSSE
## WITH SMOKED SALT

**FROM THE KITCHEN**

**SERVES** 4

Bubbly and rich chocolate mousse is taken to the next level with a pinch of smoked sea salt. Salt enhances the flavour of chocolate, making it 'pop' and intensify. It also gives a subtle crunch to the top of the dessert – and a pinch is more than enough. Smoked sea salt is available in supermarkets; it's worth keeping some in the cupboard to add a touch of smokiness to other dishes, too. Prepare this in advance and serve al fresco.

340g (12oz) silken tofu
100g (3½oz) dark chocolate (ensure dairy-free)
4 tbsp maple syrup
1 tsp good-quality vanilla extract
pinch of smoked sea salt flakes

**1** Add the silken tofu to a high-powered jug blender and blitz on high until smooth, or use a stick blender to blitz the silken tofu in a bowl.

**2** Add the dark chocolate pieces to a heatproof bowl, then melt over a pan of simmering water, making sure the base of the bowl does not touch the water. Stir occasionally until the chocolate has melted into a shiny liquid, then carefully add to the blended tofu.

**3** Stir in the maple syrup and vanilla extract and blend again to ensure the mixture is silky smooth and fully combined.

**4** Spoon into 4 ramekin dishes, then chill in the fridge for at least 4 hours or overnight until set. Just before serving sprinkle over the smoked sea salt, crushing it gently between your fingertips.

**HOT TIP**

Silken tofu can be found in most supermarkets. It's often found in the world foods aisle, instead of in the chilled section where you'll find extra-firm tofu. Silken tofu gives the mousse the soft, bubbly texture in place of eggs.

# STICKY FIGS
## WITH MAPLE-CANDIED WALNUTS AND POMEGRANATE

**BARBECUE COOKING TEMPERATURE:** medium-high heat. Move some of the charcoal to the side so part of the grill has indirect heat.

**SERVES** 4

1 tbsp vegan butter
pinch of ground cinnamon
8 ripe fresh figs, halved
6 tbsp maple syrup
2 tbsp walnuts
8 tbsp plain soya yogurt, chilled
seeds of ½ pomegranate

Also pictured on pages 26 and 76–77

Jammy, hot figs, maple-candied walnuts, cold yogurt and juicy pomegranate. Simple, natural desserts don't get much better than this. This is delicious as a sweet treat following tamarind aubergines (page 30), olive flatbreads (page 75) and pistachio, pomegranate and mint salad with bulgar and orange (page 119).

**1** Lay out two sheets of foil, large enough to stand the fig halves in. Place one on top of the other, so the figs will be double-wrapped on the grill.

**2** Melt the vegan butter for a few seconds in the microwave in a heatproof bowl, or in a small pan. Stir in the cinnamon.

**3** Brush the fig halves with the butter mix, then stand them in the foil, placing the halves together as if they are whole. Bring the sides of the foil up to the top, then pour in the maple syrup and walnuts. Scrunch the foil firmly together at the top to seal the parcel.

**4** Place the foil parcel onto the grill, over the area of indirect heat. Cook for about 15 minutes until the figs are very soft, then carefully open the top of the foil to allow the maple syrup to caramelize.

**5** Spoon the yogurt into 4 bowls.

**6** Remove the foil parcel from the barbecue and spoon the figs, walnuts and maple syrup over the yogurt. Scatter with pomegranate and serve while the figs are hot.

### HOT TIP

The figs take 15 minutes or so to cook over indirect heat on the barbecue, but it may take a little longer if the figs are firm or very large. Use tongs to gently squeeze the figs through to foil to test if they are ready – they should be very tender and have a jammy texture.

# CINDER TOFFEE

I can't get enough of cinder toffee: that crunch, those bubbles, that golden shine. And it's simpler to make than you think! Prepare up to 2 days in advance for a sweet treat that's perfect after smoked sweet potato chilli with chocolate and cinnamon (page 39), preferably under the stars.

100g (½ cup) granulated sugar
4 tbsp golden syrup
1½ tsp bicarbonate of soda (baking soda)

**1** Add the sugar and golden syrup to a large pan and cook over a high heat on the hob for 3–4 minutes without stirring. Keep a careful watch until the mixture starts to bubble and becomes the colour of maple syrup.

**2** Remove the pan from the heat and vigorously whisk in the bicarbonate of soda using a balloon whisk.

**3** Pour the frothy mixture into a shallow non-stick baking tray and leave to cool for 15–20 minutes until the top is shiny and crisp. Snap into uneven shards and pieces. Store in a dry, sealed container for up to 2 days.

**HOT TIP**

Place shards of cinder toffee into individual bags to give to guests at your barbecue – they make the perfect homemade (and very welcome) present.

# TORTILLA TURNOVERS
## WITH HOT CINNAMON APPLES

**BARBECUE COOKING TEMPERATURE:**
medium heat

**SERVES** 4

1 rounded tbsp vegan butter
4 soft white tortilla wraps
2 tsp soft light brown sugar
4 green apples, sliced
squeeze of juice from
   1 unwaxed lemon
½ tsp ground cinnamon
4 tbsp maple syrup

These tortilla turnovers have been affectionally called 'barbecue pancakes' by friends and family, because they sizzle, are buttery and sweet, and have a comforting, steamy filling. Transform simple soft tortilla wraps into a wonderful dessert with hot cinnamon apples, vegan butter and brown sugar.

**1** Melt the vegan butter in a heatproof dish in the microwave for a few seconds, or in a pan on the hob.

**2** Brush both sides of each tortilla wrap with the melted butter, then sprinkle with a pinch of brown sugar. Allow the butter to soak in while you prepare and cook the apples.

**3** Lay out two sheets of kitchen foil, large enough to securely wrap the apple slices. Lay the apple slices in the centre of one piece of foil, then squeeze over the lemon juice and sprinkle over the cinnamon. Drizzle with the olive oil, then scrunch in the foil to seal the apples. Double-wrap with the other piece of foil.

**4** Place the foil parcel onto the hot grill bars and cook for 15–20 minutes until the apples have softened and the maple syrup is bubbling.

**5** Add each tortilla wrap to the grill and cook for about 2–3 minutes on each side until just golden.

**6** Remove the foil parcel from the grill and carefully open. Place one cooked tortilla wrap onto a plate and spoon a quarter of the hot apple slices onto one side of the wrap. Fold the wrap over to make a semi-circular shape and cut into two pieces. Repeat with the other wraps and serve hot.

### HOT TIP

Green Granny Smith apple slices hold their shape well after cooking, and have a distinctive flavour, but feel free to use whatever apples you have available.

# HOT BALSAMIC STRAWBERRIES

**BARBECUE COOKING
TEMPERATURE:**
medium heat

**SERVES** 4

When you think fresh, seasonal strawberries can't get any better, try marinating them in balsamic vinegar to enhance their sweetness and colour, before grilling to caramelize them. Use skewers to make turning the strawberries easier and more even, and then serve with vegan vanilla ice cream, or a spoonful of vegan whipped cream.

4 tbsp balsamic vinegar

1 tbsp soft light brown sugar

16 strawberries, green tops removed

Pictured overleaf and on page 130

**1** In a bowl, whisk together the balsamic vinegar and brown sugar. Add the strawberries and allow to infuse for 10 minutes.

**2** Shake off the excess balsamic vinegar from the strawberries and thread 4 strawberries onto each of 4 small metal skewers.

**3** Place the skewers onto the heated grill and cook for 2–3 minutes, turning frequently until hot. Remove before the strawberries become jammy.

**4** Carefully remove the strawberries from the skewers and serve in bowls with vegan ice cream.

**HOT TIP**

I love to eat these strawberries hot from the grill, but they're also delicious when chilled after cooking and added to a simple salad.

# SANGRIA

**FROM THE KITCHEN**

**MAKES** 1 large jug

This classic Spanish punch never fails to put a smile on faces when a jug appears! Sangria tastes wonderful with grilled foods, and is a refreshing, lighter way to enjoy red wine. Serve alongside smoky paella with butter beans and olives (page 36), barbecue patatas bravas (page 86) and warm grapes with whipped cream cheese and chives (page 112).

1 unwaxed lemon, sliced

1 unwaxed orange, sliced

1 pear, thinly sliced

handful of strawberries, halved

1 x 750ml bottle of light red wine (ensure vegan)

300ml (1¼ cups) fresh orange juice, chilled

500ml (2 cups) sparkling lemonade, chilled

ice, to serve

Also pictured on pages 88–89

**1** Stir together the lemon, orange, pear and strawberries in a large jug.

**2** Pour in the red wine and orange juice, then allow to infuse for at least 1 hour or overnight to mellow in taste.

**3** Stir in the lemonade just before serving. Pour into large wine glasses filled with ice.

**HOT TIP**

Choose a light red wine for sangria, for example Pinot Noir, Merlot or Malbec, as they are low in tannins and high enough in acidity to stand up to the citrus fruit. Do note that not all wines are suitable for vegans, as animal products are often used in the production process, including isinglass (fish bladders), gelatine, cows' milk protein, and egg whites. Many supermarkets now label which of their wines are vegan, so do check before you buy.

# ENGLISH GARDEN MOCKTAIL

**FROM THE KITCHEN**

**MAKES** 1 jug

Refreshing, seasonal and served ice-cold, this long drink has grown-up flavours, without the alcohol. Choose good-quality cloudy apple juice for the tastiest mocktail. If you want to enjoy an autumnal garden mocktail, substitute the elderflower for a cinnamon stick and the sparkling lemonade for ginger ale.

¼ cucumber, sliced into rounds
4 strawberries, sliced
2 slices of unwaxed lemon
handful of fresh mint, bruised
2 sprigs of fresh elderflower
1 x 900ml bottle (scant 4 cups) of good-quality cloudy apple juice, chilled
500ml (2 cups) sparkling lemonade, chilled
crushed ice, to serve

Also pictured on pages 110–111

**1** In a large jug, muddle together the cucumber, strawberries, lemon, mint and elderflower.

**2** Pour in the apple juice, then stir in the lemonade.

**3** Serve in tall glasses over plenty of crushed ice.

**HOT TIP**

If you don't have fresh elderflower available, stir in 2 teaspoons of elderflower cordial instead.

# INDEX

# ACKNOWLEDGEMENTS

During the balmy British summer of 2021, I had the privilege of writing *Vegan BBQ* and spending each day outside developing and testing recipes. Writing recipes in the season they are intended for is a rare occurrence for a food writer, as often work is prepared months in advance, so it was my pleasure to create these recipes in the sunshine.

Firstly, I'd like to thank the editorial team at Quadrille. Huge thanks to commissioning editor Harriet Webster for believing in the project, and for your consistent dedication and attention to detail. It's always a joy to work with you! Thank you to managing director Sarah Lavelle for all of the opportunities from the very start. Special thanks to copy editor Clare Sayer for another round of prompt editorial support.

A big thank you to designer Emily Lapworth for the vision, art direction and vibrant design. I think it's my favourite to date.

Massive thanks to photographer Luke Albert, food stylist Tamara Vos and assistant Charlotte Whatcott, and prop stylist Louie Waller for the wonderful photography and styling. It was fantastic to work with you (in person!) again, between the beautiful Kent coast and south London. The photographs are everything I dreamed about for the book.

Heartfelt thanks to senior publicist Rebecca Smedley for another round of publicity. I love working with you! Thank you to marketing executive Laura Eldridge for your ongoing expertise and advice.

I am so grateful for my wonderful literary agent, Victoria Hobbs, and the hardworking team at A.M. Heath. Thank you for the chats, the laughs, the ideas, and the honest feedback. Can't wait to do it all again next time!

Thank you, as always, to my amazing friends Mary-Anne, Charlotte, Louise, Amelia, Emma, Amy, Katie, Neil and Robert. I always appreciate your texts, calls, coffees and encouragement. I owe you a balcony barbecue at mine soon.

Massive thanks to my wonderful Mum and Dad who embraced barbecue life over summer, with daily lunches (and suppers) of the dishes that made it into the book, as well as those that didn't. Thank you for cleaning the grill and washing up when I was writing up. Thank you to my fabulous sister Carolyne and brother-in-law Mark for your support and continuing to believe in me. Special thanks to Auntie May for the encouragement. Thank you as always to my clever twin nieces Tamzin and Tara for being the light of my life – I hope you enjoy adding this new book to your collection. Not forgetting the newest edition to the family, Pandi the house rabbit, who brings happiness and fun to each day.